Unchain Your Heart

Experience the Joy of Freedom

Dear Cindy,

Love you girl, Thank you so much for your support and more importantly, your friendship.

I wish you success and wild happiness!

Linda

Unchain Your Heart

Experience the Joy of Freedom

Linda Cole Dore

 RADIANT HEART PRESS

Milwaukee Wisconsin

Illustrations by Dori Gouwens.

Published by
Radiant Heart Press,
A division of HenschelHAUS Publishing, Inc.
2625 S. Greeley St. Suite 201
Milwaukee, Wisconsin 53207
www.HenschelHAUSbooks.com

All HenschelHAUS titles, imprints, and distributed
lines are available at special quantity discounts for
educational, institutional, fund-raising,
or sales promotion.

ISBN: 9781595982377
e-ISBN: 9781595982384
Library of Congress Control Number: 2013938363

Printed in the United States of America.

This book is dedicated to those who think they can't make a difference in our world and
to my grandson, Cole Matthews, who is 13 years old at the time of this writing and did make a difference.

My 84-year-old father was diagnosed with pulmonary fibrosis and put on permanent oxygen as a result of this debilitating disease. On July 1, 2013, he was doing a small repair in the basement of his home, and as he tried to shorten a screw by using a hand grinder, a spark ignited the oxygen tubes that covered his face. Cole came running down the stairs, ripped the fiery tubes from his grandfather's face, threw them on the ground, then stamped out the fire.

My dad, Arnold Cole, made a full recovery from that incident, but unfortunately, he recently lost his battle with the pulmonary fibrosis and passed away. My family and I have suffered a great loss, but will always treasure the beautiful memories of him that will forever be held in our hearts.

Cole made a life-saving difference in my father's life. It may not have added years to Dad's life, but I remember the love and sheer gratitude it placed in Dad's heart. He let Cole know exactly how grateful he was and impacting Cole's future decisions.

We can all make great life-changing decisions with a will to do so. I challenge you to live your life with intention and integrity; make waves—make the world a better place.

I love you, Dad.

Arnold Henry Cole
Born September 5, 1928
Resting in Peace August 28, 2013

Table of Contents

Acknowledgements

First and foremost, I would like to acknowledge the one who knows all, sees all and creates all—God. With guidance from the Divine, this book was inspired and the resources to help me appeared: Melissa Perdue, my life coach; Kira Henschel, my publisher, and Dori Gouwens, my illustrator. These wonderful women kept me focused on the project and moving toward the goal of completion.

I would additionally like to acknowledge Tony Robbins, inspirational author, speaker, and coach. After attending his event, "Unleash the Power Within," a new sense of commitment and possibility was "unleashed" and I began to write this book.

My Facebook friends were also a great source of help. Whenever I was at a loss coming up with characters to write about, they would come to the rescue with their ideas—thank you.

I would also like to acknowledge my friend, John Rachford. Over twenty years ago, he saw something in me and encouraged me through his mentoring to be the best I could be, even when I did not believe it.

Thanks to my family: Arnold and Dorothy Cole, for without you, Dad and Mom, I would not be here. My daughters, Tina Dore and Marsha Paladino—I thank you for your open ears listening to all the ramblings from me during the course of creating this book.

I am very blessed to have such supportive and caring people in my life. Thank you for being my friends.

Linda Cole Dore
Chicago, Illinois
2013

Preface

I am writing this book just for you. Have you ever felt like you were in prison without hope of ever seeing daylight again? Maybe you haven't experienced physical prison, but the one you have created with negative experience can seem just as confining. Often when we find ourselves living in this state of being, it is hard to see an escape route, or it seems like too much effort to try and change our attitude. This can be a death sentence if that is what you choose. This book is to show you that there are options to change your state of being and they are all within you, free for the asking.

The walls you have created took many years to build. Now the prison in which your being resides cannot grow; it must remain restricted because that is what you have told it to do.

Have I ever been in prison? Not physically, but within my mind I have. Change never came until I hit rock bottom and realized there was only one direction to go that would offer any relief. When the pain gets great enough that the soul cannot tolerate it any more, it will change directions at your choosing. In other words, a new choice is made.

I do not profess to know what you are feeling right now, for that is up to you. It is your choice, one that no one can take away from you without your permission. If you choose to feel victimized, that is your right; if you choose to feel defeated, that is your right; if you choose to be angry, that is your right. You can also choose to accept the place you are in life and grow from it. That also is your right. When the feeling of hitting the absolute bottom comes, it could be the most miraculous moment of your life. Focus your attention on all that is possible ahead of you, which is just about every-thing when you are sitting on the floor. If you ask yourself how you are feeling in this present moment serves you, you may find that a better choice will serve you positively rather than negatively.

In this book, I will take you on a journey through crippling states and show you how to escape the limitations each one places on you. Close your eyes for a minute and try to visualize a heart with heavy chains wrapped around it, weighing it down. Feel the weight that puts on you. Now see the heart becoming bigger and bigger until the chains can no longer confine it and break apart, releasing the heavy load your heart has been carrying for so long. Feel the difference in how you feel—that is the difference between a chained heart and one that is let free. That, my friend, is the breakthrough I hope to give you in this book.

Our lives are a series of experiences and how we react to them will determine whether we grow and live, or stagnate and have a death experience. Admittedly, when we are at the bottom, our surroundings are not growth-oriented. However, we have complete and positive control over the inner choices of how to feel and respond to challenges. That is one freedom we can count on. What we do with those choices is up to each of us individually.

At this time, I would like to introduce you to Jo—not Joseph, nor Josephine, just your average Jo.

Jo represents you and me and will guide you through both the positive and negative mindsets we so often experience throughout our lives.

Your average "Jo"

Everyone has his or her own story. I do not know your story, but I do know mine and I know that whatever you want to change about yourself, you can. You simply must decide to do so and focus on the result of who you wish to become. There is always hope, with the help of God—you can change your heart and enjoy a peaceful, joyous life. I am not saying it will be easy, but it is definitely worth the effort.

Good Luck!

The Voice of Choice

The Voice of Choice

Consider what the world wo be like if we did not have the ay to choose. The Supreme powe God, Buddha, or whatever that may be you, allows us the ability to make chs by utilizing our free will to do this that, think this or that, or feel this or tl Free will is a gift, and when we make right decisions that move us forward our relationship with the Universe, wperience peace. Making a choice thattricts growth and life will not move usward, and fear and anxiety will be tresult. Fear and anxiety are life-endinr they stagnate and cripple our efforts grow. Everything we think, do, or feel choice we must make to act oneay or the other.

Choice is decision. Sho I or shouldn't I? Without decisonse mind wans in all directions and can get lost in t overwhelming options. So what doeske control of a given situation? You by making a decision and taking actio'he opportunity to make a choice is a ierful moment for us. We are on the v: of changing or reaffirming who we ar the result of the next decision.

If approach each choice with an open nd and consider the conse-quencf the choice before deciding, we can ce positive experiences through that don. If we have a history of fear, it can more difficult to make choices and if are afraid to choose, then it is possibl sabotage our future by indeci-sion. N people react to their history habitua without considering that they can che the situation's outcome by makingbetter choice. When doing so, we aligourselves with the positive energy veserve.

Thro the events in our lives, choices e been made for us and we have majur own choices—the result of all thosecices is the person we are at the present moment. Recognizing the pivotal point when a decision is in front of us, followed by evaluating the effect that each choice would have on the situation, and the action of making a choice will expand our knowledge of who we are. Whether it serves us well or not adds to who we are through the experience of our choices. Choice plus action mean life.

The Power of the Tongue

It is easy to say things that lift people up or crush their spirits. After observing others for many years, it has occurred to me that we are more prone to negative thoughts because negative is easier than positive. Why? It is because we are pro-grammed from childhood through the use of the word "no." Surely our parents and peers meant well and were trying to protect us, but the fact of the matter is that saying "no" cuts off experience. Each thought we have when communicated to another immediately invokes a negative connotation in their mind because of this conditioning.

Think of a two-year-old child learning about life through his parents' watchful eye. If the child tries to touch a hot stove, the mother says "no" to protect him. Do not cry, do not run, do not touch, and on and on and on. If you kept a record of how many times you used the words "no" or "yes" in a day—whether to yourself or to others, you would be amazed in the result.

The road less traveled is to instill positive reinforcement in each other and overcome the negative preconditioning. All of the choices that the parents are making for their child are meant to keep that child safe and happy; they just need to reinforce those choices positively rather than negatively. "No" is not necessarily a bad decision, but if "no" is the best choice, give an explanation of why "no" will benefit the situation at hand. The toddler who is about to grab a hot pot from the stovetop does not know that he is in danger, so by telling him not to touch that because it will hurt and cause him pain will let him know that out of love, the parents are guiding him to a better choice, thus becoming a positive experience rather than negative.

We have been given the privilege of possessing free will, which gives us the opportunity to choose who we become. When we communicate love and kindness to others, positive energy is put out into the Universe. One small word can change lives forever—such as "yes" or "no." It can strip away hope or create confidence that will alter not only an individual life, but the future of the world as we know it.

* * * * *

Mother Teresa made a decision when she was twelve years of age to become a nun and devote her life to Jesus Christ. She said "yes" to God. At age eighteen, she left her home in Albania and traveled to India where her work began. Each day, as she walked through the streets of Calcutta, she encountered tens of thousands of sick or dying people who lived in extreme poverty. One day, she encountered a young girl who was lying semi-conscious in the middle of the rubbish and filth, with hungry rats waiting for her to die. It was then that she made a decision to say "yes" to help these impoverished people and "no" to her more comfortable life as a nun in the order in which she served.

Mother Teresa picked up the young girl and brought her to the local hospital and received a less-than-welcome reception upon her arrival. Through her great love of these people and persistence, the hospital finally did agree to treat the girl and this was the beginning of the pilgrimage of the greatest missionary we have seen in recent times. She devoted her entire life of eighty-seven years to making life better for "the least of these," which were Jesus' words of how to serve humanity.

Mother Teresa made many good choices in her lifetime, but each good choice she made brought her closer to knowing her true heart. She did not achieve the Nobel Peace Prize and all of the other humanitarian awards from her work instantly; it was though good choice after good choice year after year.

* * * * *

The first good choice you make can lead you on an extraordinary path as well. It can be easier than you think to change. Just say "yes" to the good and "no" to the bad.

If we think before we speak and set some guidelines for what we say before we say it, we speak wisely. The power of the words we speak define who we are. When you say something hurtful to someone, you are verbalizing what is inside of you.

Sometimes something comes out of your mouth that is shameful and you might think "I don't know where that came from." Yes, you do know where that came from; it is who you are at that moment. For example, boasting about skills or accomplishments communicates to others that you are experiencing insecurity and you need reassurance from them that what you are telling them is true. Sometimes the need to be right can make one feel that one is better than others. By the way, one isn't.

Contrarily, if you degrade your abilities and communicate that to others, then you are also indicating that you are experiencing insecurity that you are not as good as they are—and by the way, YOU ARE!

We as humans can be everything we want to be with decision, focus and action. When we give praise to others, an immediate change in their demeanor occurs and an inner glow radiates through their expression. If we can affect a change like that in others, why don't we do it more often? Why don't we give ourselves praise?

You know how good if feels when someone is kind to you, so concentrate on spreading the goodness. Pay it forward. Remember to think before you speak and the results you will experience will amaze you. Consider if they are kind words, are they true words and will they lead to a good outcome? These are the questions that will help you make the right choices every time. If, after answering these questions, you come up with no tangible benefit of what you are considering saying, don't say it. Sometimes not saying something is much more empowering than saying it. The guidelines you establish for decision making will help you travel the road to a better you. Choose your words wisely and keep that tongue under control and life will be a much more pleasurable journey.

Focus and Determination

Focus and Determination

Now we are getting to the good stuff, the stuff that can change a life from sadness and failure to one of joy and success.

Focus and determination are related, but not the same. The definition of focus, for the purpose of this chapter, is "selectively concentrating on one aspect of the environment while ignoring other things."

The definition of determination is "firmness of purpose, will or intention," and when you combine determination with focus, this can help you achieve almost anything in life.

Let's talk about focus first. Our minds tend to lead us in many directions all at once, which can make it difficult to concentrate on an individual action we would like to accomplish. Distraction leads us nowhere except in circles. To focus on an outcome we want to achieve, we must stand up to our scatterbrained mind, decide to block out the opposing thoughts, and choose thoughts related to the outcome we wish to achieve. The outcome becomes the focus of our attention, which is the beginning of the solution.

A recent article about Barack Obama that appeared in *Vanity Fair* magazine gives an interesting take on how to make focusing easier. I would have never come up with this simple and easy little mind trick, but then I am not the president of the United States either. Obama was asked why he had the decorative plates in the White House taken down. His answer was simply, "I am not a plate type of guy." He chose to eliminate the plates from his life because they added no meaning to it, so why should he look at them? They only added a distraction and kept him from focusing on what was important to him. That might have been a small action, but it simplified what was before him. Similarly, he chooses to only wear black and blue suits to avoid the distraction of focusing on what he wears. By doing this, he is conserving his decision-making energy for bigger, more important things that need his full attention.

We all can get caught up in the minutia that our minds dish out, and it is exhausting to hash over the details of trivia. Simply ask yourself if all these interrupting thoughts are helping you achieve the end result you desire. If the answer is no, then change your thoughts. By not allowing them to become the focus of your attention, you can create the path of your choosing. Doesn't that sound much more enjoyable that wandering around without a purpose? I don't know about you, but the mere thought of being scatterbrained drains the life out of me and is just plain boring after a while.

> *If people knew how hard I worked to get my mastery, it wouldn't seem so wonderful after all.*
> —Michelangelo

One of the best examples of a focused person I can come up with is Walter Payton, who was an incredibly talented running back for the Chicago Bears . He was brought up in a small town in

Mississippi, the son of a factory worker along with his brothers and sisters. His parents raised their family with strong faith in God and discipline that instilled a great sense of values in their children. They always told their children that they could achieve anything that they wanted to if they put their heart and soul into their effort. Walter said that statement was his ticket to the Super Bowl.

> *Where there is a will, there is a way.*
> —English Proverb

When there is something compelling enough to make or break your life, you set the course and begin the journey. Walter's training regimens were said to be brutal, almost torturous, but with his laser-sharp focus on building his body into a fine-tuned football gladiator, he became one of the greatest players that football has ever known.

You never know what is going to inspire you. Look at Walter—a simple sentence set his path on a journey of awesome greatness that will live in the hearts of everyone forever.

It may seem like a stretch from where you are right now, and it is—but we all know that stretching is one of the best things you can do for a body. If you apply the stretching theory to your mind and heart, imagine the effects that you could orchestrate? Find what is important to you, what you enjoy, at what you excel. When you hit on the right thing, you will know it. All of a sudden, related thoughts will begin to come and questions will flood your head that link to "the focus."

The brain responds to inspiration and when you find it and want it to become a part of you, the next step is to make it real: it will change from a want to a must. It is now time to become determined that this new focus WILL be on the outcome you desire.

The best example of determination and focus I can give you are the events that took place during the Apollo 13 space mission. On April 11, 1970, the seemingly successful launch from Cape Kennedy sent the three astronauts on their way to their goal of landing on the moon. Undetected problems occurred during the initial liftoff. These occurrences would later cause a catastrophic explosion of an oxygen tank in the service module, which led to the famous quote, "Houston, we have a problem." That was an understatement.

The explosion put not only the moon landing in jeopardy, but the lives of the three courageous astronauts aboard the space ship. The problems that arose from the explosion included a severely damaged service module, limited hydrogen and oxygen supplies, and other functions necessary for water and electrical sources for operation of the ship, as well as life support for its crew. Adding to the drama was the time element, or lack thereof.

Back on the ground at NASA headquarters, the Apollo 13 support team was facing the gravity of a very complicated and unchartered problem that needed master ingenuity under extreme pressure. This is where teamwork was at its best. There were many issues that needed resolving, but one by one, the team conquered each challenge with dedication and focus on the task at hand and determination to achieve a successful outcome for this Apollo 13 mission.

On April 17, 1970, the successful splash-down in the Pacific Ocean culminated this extraordinary collaboration. Though the moon landing had to be aborted, this mission turned out to be one of the most successful instances of what humankind is capable of when necessary.

> *You have enormous untapped power that you will probably never tap, because most people never run far enough on their first wind to ever find they have a second.*
> —William James

What the Apollo 13 mission shows us is that if you know in advance the outcome you wish to achieve, your focus becomes more defined. What you focus on is what you shall receive, and I believe that is true. If you focus on negative aspects or outcomes, then that is what you will receive. However, if you place your sights on what is good and positive, then your life will change for the good.

Another example of determination is when Abraham Lincoln, the sixteenth president of the United States, set his mind on abolishing slavery. With all his being he believed that was the right thing to do. His inspiration was accompanied by his faith and guidance from God.

The odds of obtaining the majority vote required to approve the Emancipation Proclamation were slim at best in the beginning of his quest. In the push to obtain these votes, he focused on the key members of his inner circle to find solutions that would lead to the majority vote required to pass this new amendment. One by one minds were changed to vote "yea" instead of "nay" for this historical legislation to become law. All of this maneuvering took place in a mere month and when it came time for the vote, the momentum that Lincoln had built changed the lives of all people living in the United States of America. Freedom belongs to everyone.

Determination is based on the excitement and motivation you have for your focus. To achieve anything you must have motivation, not just a little bit of enthusiasm for the result. Get excited about it. Imagine all the ways your life will improve when you attain this outcome. When a book inspires us to take action, such as go on a diet or train for a marathon, we feel momentum start to build. Feel the joy that comes with succeeding. This is the state of being you want to be in when you are working toward the desired outcome. You can put yourself in this state at will, just as you did here. Feed your mind with passionate thoughts that move you forward in your quest and success will be yours.

Courage

Courage

Courage is a virtue we all wish to have. Without courage, humanity would cease to exist. From early childhood, we have developed our courageous instincts to become more proficient in skills and thoughts. Think about an infant learning to walk. If he or she did not get up again after falling the first time, would the child ever walk? If during the first attempt, the child experienced pain from the fall, would it not take courage to get up and try again, knowing it might hurt?

Courage is facing adversity guided by the righteousness of physical and moral behavior. Throughout the course of our lives, we learn the difference between what is right and wrong and develop a belief system that becomes our moral guide. When a person or event comes along that challenges a belief we hold to be right, an action to substantiate that belief comes to the surface to be confirmed or denied. Confirming the belief we hold takes courage because it is in opposition to the person or event before us. It involves bravery, perseverance, and grace.

I am writing this chapter the day after the 11th anniversary of 9/11/2001. It is appropriate to speak of the courage it took to respond to such a horrific national disaster. The firemen, policemen, doctors, nurses and all the people who reached out and helped our country get through that awful event deserve our utmost respect and gratitude. Many heroes rose to the occasion that day, and here is the story of one of them.

Todd Beamer

It has been eleven years since Todd's heroic actions were called to our attention. He was a good man who loved his family and had a great life ahead of him.

As a young boy, he chose sports to teach him about excellence and teamwork and carried those lessons with him for the rest of his short life. He grew up in a Christian home and when he met his wife, Lisa, they continued with their Christian faith. Todd was an account manager for an Internet database company in New Jersey and was required to travel quite a bit. Little did he know when he kissed his wife and boys goodbye that morning, he would never see them again.

After Todd's flight took off, the hijackers went into action. The pilot and copilot were stripped of their control of the plane and locked out of the cabin. Chaos ensued and passengers began to communicate with their loved ones and emergency units via cell and airphones and found out the World Trade Center and Pentagon had been attacked. Todd was on the phone with an operator when the realization hit that the end of all their lives was coming fast. Knowing this, a group of passengers, among them Todd, plotted to storm the cockpit to foil the plans of the hijackers to deliver another devastating blow to our country.

The last memory the operator had of her conversation with Todd was the group's recitation of the Lord's Prayer and the words, "Are you guys ready? Let's roll". Then the explosion. Then silence.

Courage is the action of being brave in a time of uncertainty without fear of harm. The group of men who stormed the cockpit knew their fate, but out of love for their country and all of humanity, they acted with unwavering courage as their last experience on this earth.

When you are fearful of a situation, look at the options you have, foresee the possible outcome, and take action toward the outcome you desire. Knowing what you wish to achieve gives you confidence, which allows you to feel courageous, which in turn allows you to take action without fear. When your heart and mind are aligned to perform feats that over-come a fearful situation, a change occurs that improves your life. If your heart and mind are not aligned, there is no change and fear remains—no growth occurs. All of us have the ability to be courageous and when we choose the right direction, we can affect positive change.

Mattie Stepanek

When Mattie was three years old, he began to write poetry. Yes, I said three, so you know he was an extraordinary being from the start. The inspiration came from the death of his brother as a means to cope with his feelings.

Mattie's older brother had just passed away from a rare form of muscular dystrophy. His diagnosis led to the discovery that all the Stepanek children had the same destiny. This discovery was made after the birth of Jeni Stepanek's four children. That fate included herself as well. She said that Mattie's purpose for being on this earth was "to be a messenger, to make people smile despite their challenges." And that he did.

Mattie's view of life was from a wheelchair with the use of a breathing tube. He was a poet, philosopher, and peacemaker. He did not focus on his illness, but rather on what he could do to inspire others to live the best life possible, no matter what the circumstances. Throughout his young life, he appeared on the Oprah Winfrey show, Good Morning America, and Larry King Live, and met his all-time hero, Jimmy Carter. He made numerous appearances worldwide promoting his cause. During this time, he underwent many dangerous surgeries associated with this rare disease. His courage came from his mission in life: to help others gain peace no matter what the situation is. Spreading that message made the tiny warrior tick.

Eventually Mattie's frail little body gave out and he died in 2004, just before his 14th birthday, joining his three other siblings in the afterlife. What a special soul Mattie Stepanek was. His fate in life did not define him; his service to help others did. He helped so many people lead a more fulfilling life. One of the most beautiful rewards is the joy of helping the world become a better place.

Within each of us is a place we can find peace and when realized, we can be assured a freedom that no one can take away from us unless we give them permission to do so. When you allow others to influence or intimidate your peace, fear comes and peace fades.

Courage takes patience and faith in God. Though often it is difficult to know that God is there for you in fearful times, if you keep the faith intact with your heart and soul focused on the Lord, peace will prevail. Along with patience, you can remain courageous.

Jesus Christ, the Father of Courage

The Bible tells us that we are to follow the ways that Jesus has shown us. Jesus never took the easy way or the most popular way; He followed God His Father's way, the Divine Will that God has for all of his children. Whether you believe the existence of God or not, you must acknowledge that the biblical renditions of His courage are amazing. Jesus knew what His fate was for all of

His life here on earth and did not flinch at His destiny. That took courage.

He performed many miracles to show us that following Him would produce great fruit in life. Jesus healed the lame, gave sight to the blind, walked on water, and died a brutal, tortuous death on the cross to save us from our sinful nature. The night before He was to die on the cross, He struggled with His upcoming fate and asked His Father if there was another way, but God responded for Him to remain faithful and that He would be with Him now and forever.

> *In the world, you will have trouble but take courage, for I have conquered the world.*
> —Jesus Christ

This is such an important symbolic message to us upon which we can rely in our times of great despair. The things that we have no control of can be faced with courage and dignity by trusting in God and His plan for us if we follow His lead. What feels like the end of the world to us is not; our lives continue.

How you handle the situations in the life you have been given is what's important, not the outcome. The outcome will be what God intends for you if you follow His divine guidance, and that will give you peace in your heart.

Confinement

Confinement

The definition of confinement is imprisonment, limitation, restriction, restraint. We can be physically confined by the walls of a prison, self-limitations such as mental walls we created that limit our thinking, or limitations created by others and imposed on us, such as being confined to bed rest by a doctor.

Let's look at the realities of confinement. When you are confined, you have limited freedoms, but you also have limited responsibility for your physical existence. When confined, you have more time to focus on your personal beliefs, but you have limited ability to repair the beliefs that are not serving you well. This can be done by choosing to think differently than you have in the past. There have been many great leaders who have not only endured their physical confinement, but have turned it into a means to make their lives better.

John McCain

Take John McCain, for example. McCain was a pilot in the Navy during the Viet Nam war and on his 23rd attack mission, when his plane was hit and began to spiral out of control. He was ejected from the plane and dropped into a lake, where he was badly injured, breaking bones and incurring internal injuries. Unable to use his arms, he managed to pull the inflation control on his life vest with his teeth. When found by the North Vietnamese soldiers, he was spat on, kicked, and beaten with gun butts and was near death. He was put in the "Hanoi Hilton," a prison, with the rest of the prisoners of war. Badly in need of medical treatment, his captors required him to give military information in trade for treatment— McCain refused and then the torture began.

Eventually, his conditions were so intolerable that he agreed to give information if they would give him medical treatment. His plan was to hold them off so he could get into a hospital. Once in the hospital, the doctors said it was a useless attempt because he was going to die. The North Vietnamese began interrogating him and he gave limited information. When asked to give the names of the men in his squadron, he named the offensive line of the Green Bay Packers.

During this time, the North Vietnamese found out that McCain's father was a top admiral in the U.S. Navy and only then did they decide to give him medical treatment, which was shoddy at best. They decided to use McCain as a publicity ploy and portray him as a traitor to his country and the world.

The torturous treatments continued while he was still in the hospital, A news report was made of McCain lying in his body cast, smoking cigarettes as if he were being treated as a prince receiving the best of treatment. His captors offered him a conditional release because of his father's position, which they viewed as one of the military elite. John turned down the offer because he did not want this special treatment at the expense of deserting his fellow POWs. The North Vietnamese took that as a slap in the face, and McCain was told that things were going to get really bad for him.

At that point, he was thrown into solitary confinement and remained there for two more years with daily beatings and numerous other methods of torture. His total time in confinement was five and a half years.

The POW's release came after the escalation of the United States military force rendered their negotiations more of a reality. In the spring of 1972, the final release agreements were signed and on March 15, 1972, John McCain walked across the tarmac and stepped on to a U.S. plane that would take him home.

When later asked how he had survived, John McCain cited his faith in his country, his Naval family and God. He did not become bitter and so engrossed in his ordeal as a POW that he let it define who he was as a person. McCain took the experience and turned it into a brilliant career and even wrote about the injustices of the Code of Conduct in Viet Nam, a paper which was used as a guide-line in revamping the U.S. Code of Conduct.

> *The real glory is being knocked to your knees and then coming back. That's real glory. That's the essence of it.*
> —Vince Lombardi

Can you imagine the profound effect those changes might have made? Do you think his experience as a POW led him to have a more meaningful impact on the world and for future POWs?

* * * * *

Our most devastating experiences can be the most meaningful if we use the capacity to create value in not only existence, but that of humanity. Being physically confined gives us the ability to focus on the truth of who we are and what our purpose is in this world.

One of the most important questions you can ask yourself, "What do I want?" When you come up with your answer, you have an outcome. When you know your outcome, ask yourself, "Why do I want it?" and when you know the purpose of the outcome you desire and if it aligns with God's plan for you, all things are possible.

Pastor Lonnie

Pastor Lonnie came rolling into my life about five years ago, and when he did, I wondered how he ended up on a wheelchair. When I asked him that question, he smiled and said, "God had a different plan for my life than I did." He grew up on a farm in Texas with his family and thought his future would be in agriculture as well. Lonnie was a happy kid and always had a smile on his face. He was tall like his father and liked basketball and all the other sports his friends enjoyed. After he attended his first Bible camp, he had heard a tiny whisper that led him to believe God wanted him to be a pastor. He was very excited about this and told his buddies of this revelation, but to his dismay, they were not of the same opinion. As often happens in teenage years, they started making fun of this silly ambition and Lonnie gave in to the peer pressure.

Off to college he went to study agriculture. After one year of school, on September 8th, 1974, Lonnie's life took a drastic turn. He was in a severe car crash, which crushed three of his vertebrae and left him paralyzed from the waist down—he was nineteen years old. He was far from home in a hospital bed and had plenty of time to process what this would mean for his life. Again that whisper came and this time Lonnie was listening. He knew at that moment that God wanted him to become faithful and serve him, but first he had plenty of rehabilitation on his crippled body that needed to be done. With great determination and a lot of hard work, Lonnie was back in school the following semester, but this time he was in school for a new career, a Christian calling.

In 1974, the world wasn't as accessible for handicapped folks and it wasn't as easy to get around. But the bigger adjustment Lonnie had to deal with was how people perceived him. Being in a wheelchair made him different now, and he admitted that when he had not been handicapped, he avoided contact with anyone who was, for it was uncomfortable. Now he was the handicapped person and knew what it felt like to be avoided. He could have felt self-pity or anger, but Lonnie chose to make his situation an opportunity to create a comfortable bridge for understanding others.

My next question for Lonnie was, "Did you ever feel sorry for yourself or angry with God?"

Without hesitation, he answered, "No, I never questioned God on my fate. I did feel sad at times, and we all do. When I saw my friends playing basketball and knew I could never do that again, that made me sad. There is a big difference between feeling sad and experiencing self-pity. Sadness is momentary, self-pity is mentally confining. Sadness can lead to self-pity if you let it. You cannot grow in self-pity. When you are sad, you can experience the loss of something and move on."

> *Others can stop you temporarily; only you can do it permanently.*
> —Don Ward

I asked him if he experienced being fearful about what this would mean in his life, and if so, what was he afraid of. He told me that he did have fears: he feared that no one would ever love him because of his handicap and he feared his handicap would limit his opportunities for his life.

"We are all fearful at times, but I put my faith in the Lord and as always, the peace of his presence in my life was sufficient," Pastor Lonnie explained.

You will be happy to know that Lonnie did in fact find love, get married, and finished college, overcoming what others viewed as a handicap. There were limited opportunities for clergy in a wheelchair at that time and he needed to work and go to plan B. He sent out resume after resume with few responses, so it was time to expand his horizons again.

For the next thirteen years, Lonnie worked in the insurance industry and as a corporation manager, not exactly what he wanted to do with his life. A blessing in disguise came when the company he worked for went out of business and he again was looking for a job. The resumes flew out regularly; but this time they went to churches throughout the country, and again, received little or no response.

Then one day in 1994, a response came from the pastor of a church in

Illinois. Lonnie knew what his future was —finally an opportunity to serve God. He and his wife have been there ever since that fateful letter arrived in the mail.

Lonnie turned his confinement in the wheelchair to a life of joy and peace, not only for himself, but for thousands of other folks whom he inspires on a daily basis. The plan Pastor Lonnie had for his life was certainly different than God's intention.

Looking a devastating event in the eye and deciphering the truth that God is trying to show you may be hard to face. Was it easy? Definitely not. Can it be done? Definitely yes. Is it worth it? You can do it.

Jaycee Dugard

In 1991, an eleven-year-old girl was walking to school when a car stopped and asked her for directions. The man behind driving the car quickly zapped her with a stun gun, immobilizing her so he could stash her in the back of his car. The girl was not sure where he took her, but she knew it took a long time to get there. This man had a partner to help him kidnap this young girl—his wife. The girl was Jaycee Dugard.

Once they reached the destination, they took Jaycee inside to show her the ropes of what was to come. For the next eighteen years, she was the victim of not only sexual abuse, but of moral, physical, and mental abuse as well. They stripped her of her childhood and brought her to motherhood by age fourteen. She was confined to a small room in a shed and handcuffed to a bed. There were no windows to know if it was day or night. Jaycee was dependent on the couple for food to be brought in and had to hold her bodily functions until a bucket was brought for her to relieve herself. She was alone almost all of the time, in solitary confinement.

As the weeks turned into months and the months into years, the young girl was extremely lonely and the captors took full advantage of that by making her dependent upon them for human contact. She began to actually look forward to seeing them, as skewed as the relationship was.

During her imprisonment she never gave up hope that someday she would be free. She remained grateful that she was alive and tried to make her situation tolerable by living in her present moment, because that is what she was allowed to do.

Was she fearful? You bet. Each time she heard the keys jiggle the lock of her confinement, she feared the consequences, but she also feared that if the door did not open, she would not eat. She figured out that if she cooperated with the system, she would receive more privileges to make her life a little easier. She never relinquished her soul to them, though. She occupied her mind with lists of her favorite things, favorite places, favorite activities, and those of her family for those were thoughts that nourished her life. Those thoughts kept her alive and growing.

Eventually, she did get her freedom in 2009 and she and her two daughters are now learning to navigate living outside of confinement, which has not been not easy for them. They had been dependent on their captors for everything, so each choice they now had was a fearful one. Jaycee was still mentally confined and needed and still receives therapy to help her shed those fears.

After her release, it was discovered that Phillip Girrado was a convicted sex offender who took mind-altering drugs to further cloud his already messed-up mind. Toward the end of Jaycee's captivity, it became almost a game for him to bring her and the two girls out in public because he knew that they were confined mentally as well. But someone noticed that something was not right and pointed it out to the officials, which led to the discovery of his evil secret. The tables now turned and Girrado would become the prisoner—for 431 years.

The appalling story became big news and the media surrounded her every move trying to capture a photo or the answers to their many personal questions. She now felt another type of confinement: limited ability to go about her life freely without everyone hounding her. The last thing she wanted was to be in the public eye, for she had had no human contact for eighteen years except for that of the kidnappers.

What good could possibly come out of such an awful confinement? Jaycee has written a book about her experiences. Her purpose is to call attention to kidnapping and child slavery. It can inspire others to help change the outcome for those who survive and aid the parents of the victims. She has developed a foundation to do just that. Did Jaycee turn the ordeal of her confinement into encouragement for others? What is your motivation to help others avoid the confinement of your life?

Nelson Mandela

The last story I will share with you is about a man who spent 27 years of his life in prison and became one of the greatest leaders this world has ever known. Born in 1918, his real name was *Rolihlahla,* or "troublemaker." He was the first member of his family to attend school. His teacher decided that his name should be "Nelson."

In 1948, the South African election victory supported the apartheid policy of racial segregation, which inspired Mandela to become politically active. Nelson Mandela's life was greatly influenced by that of Mohandas Gandhi, who had also served time in prison for his beliefs of nonviolent approach of resistance, or non-cooperation, in India.

In 1964, Mandela was arrested and charged with sabotage and treason. He was found guilty and imprisoned for twenty-seven years under the most basic conditions. He served hard labor with limited privileges. He was considered a "Class D" prisoner, which meant that he received the least of privileges. He focused on studying for his Bachelor of Law, degree which he received from the University of London through a correspondence program. He could have chosen to be angry or feel sorry for himself, but he chose growth (life) over stagnation (death).

In February 1985, Mandela was offered his freedom on the condition that he "unconditionally reject his political positions." He informed his captors that he would not agree to relinquish his beliefs in exchange for personal freedom. Mandela indeed rejected the offer, releasing a statement via his daughter saying "What freedom am I being offered while the organization of the people remains banned? Only free men can negotiate. A prisoner cannot enter into contracts." Mandela knew that if he agreed to this offer, he would be able to exist outside the bars, but would still be imprisoned by the lack of freedom he so strongly supported. Eventually he was released and became one of the greatest leaders in the world.

Had Mandela chosen to constrict his thoughts and actions with anger, pity or violence for the twenty-seven years he was in prison, an entire country would never have known the quality of life they now enjoy. Mandela's choices of learning and maintaining his integrity during his imprisonment created enormous change in not only his country, but the world as well. Your life can have the equally profound impact that each of these individuals have had in the world. Having the conviction to make good choices no matter what circumstances you are experiencing will allow you freedom, even if you are confined physically. Your freedom starts with the next choice you make. Do you want to dwell on the conditions in which you are actually confined, or do you want to feel the anticipation of creating a great life? Each decision you are faced with offers

Together we will work to support courage where there is fear, foster agreement where there is conflict, and inspire hope where there is despair.
—Nelson Mandela

you a fresh start, so challenge yourself—turn your confinement into something that inspires freedom. It is not always easy, but we all know that anything of value must be earned.

Anger

Anger Kills

Anger is a strong feeling of grievance and displeasure that constricts the ability to be. It can be caused from suppression, which limits or "kills" by means of destruction and defeats growth; or it can be caused by oppression, which is domination or persecution of beliefs that conflict with yours. Anger causes stress, fear, worry, health problems, and a multitude of other negative, self-crippling behaviors. The choice to be angry closes all the pathways to living a healthy life, both physically, mentally, and emotionally.

Where does anger come from? Anger comes from internalizing experiences that are in conflict with our personal belief system. Each choice we have made in life, from infancy to the present moment, defines our beliefs. Some of us may have similar beliefs, but most likely, we are unique in who we are by the choices we have made. When a situation arises that clashes with our self-imposed belief of who we are, there is another choice that confronts us—we can either accept that the other has the right to believe whatever he or she thinks, or not accept that belief and continue with trying to force your belief of what is right on them. If the latter option is what you choose, anger has just found its birthright and you have issued a death certificate to any growth of relationship with that individual.

The anger being generated in that moment not only takes its toll on the individual with whom you are in conflict, but also caused great harm to you. Did you ever notice that when you are angry that your heart beats faster? How about what happens to your muscles? Do you feel their constriction and tensing? Not to mention the negative energy that radiates throughout your body, mind and makes its way into the external world.

So how do you diffuse your anger? The most outstanding news I can tell you is that you can change how you feel. Once you understand that anger is an emotion you feel and not who you are, the journey to the root of the feeling becomes less threatening. You are not an emotion—you are a human being who has had experiences that have shaped your beliefs.

Before you can understand the "how" to overcome anger, you must find the "why." It's time to roll up your sleeves and begin the work.

Every situation can result in two separate and opposing points of view without resulting in a dispute. Anger originates when the conflict cannot be resolved or accepted by the other. The other person feels the need to defend his or her opinion as right and make the other wrong.

When you try to force your belief as the right belief on another, you are invalidating the other person's right to have a different belief, which puts negative rather than positive energy in the world. The better choice is to accept that you and the other have opposing beliefs and respect that he or she is just as entitled to those feelings or beliefs. Such an approach will not only leave the door open for a continued relationship, it will also show the other that you respect his or her personal truths as well.

Anger is not always the result of conflict with another person. It can also be self-directed. If your current life situation is not the life you wish to live, often reflection of the past choices that brought you to the present will flood the present, which eliminates the possibility of growth. By reliving this self-inflicted choice to live out your past mistakes again, the anger resurfaces and becomes the reaffirming force of your unhappiness. This justifies your "right" to be angry. I don't know about you, but the cost of being right becomes much more than I am willing to pay. It just isn't worth the energy.

So if you feel you need to be "right," you are sitting with your anger and feeling smug because you have validated that it is your right to be angry. It doesn't feel too good, does it? This is the moment that you must acknowledge in order to overcome the need to be right. When you can release that need to be right, you are moving (taking action) forward to engage with life again.

Anger is an emotion we all feel at some point in our lives and it is how we handle it that really matters. How do you express your anger? Are you a "spewer" or a "stewer"?

When angered, do you immediately blurt out a response when someone says something to you that you disagree with before taking time to consider what was said? If this is the case, then you are a "spewer." When you spontaneously react to conflict, it may momentarily relieve your anxiety, but you are also transferring that anxiety to the person with whom you are communicating. When you explode, there is always a negative reaction that will only escalate negativity in the present moment. The more violent your reaction, the more negative energy strengthens in a conflict making the present extremely dangerous. The two parties in a spewing conflict are always trying to "one up" the other to dominate the other. Spewing without thought can and does add discouraging energy to relationships.

If you are a "stewer," rather than exploding and spewing all over the other when in conflict, you neatly tuck the evidence in a mental file to be used at a later time so you can prove you are right. Over time, all the ingredients simmer internally until you feel it is cooked perfectly. When doing this, you think you are avoiding confrontation by not voicing your opposition in the present, but in reality, you are compiling the evidence with other similar records in your arsenal to use when the moment is right. Some-times the arsenal becomes so overloaded with ammunition, it accidentally explodes when least expected. This way of handling anger can be just as dangerous as spewing. Going through life with this heavy load inside of you makes decisions much harder to make and all those records that you have been stashing in those mental files are not the best source of reference when making choices anyway. If you make a decision using those references, it surely will not remedy the situation. You may be able to prove your point, but you won't improve the relationship with that person.

Stewers and spewers have a lot in common. They like to feel right, they are prideful, they feel justified in their anger, and they are unwilling to accept change. Whichever tendency you may see in yourself, try and find a way to diffuse it because anger will suck the life out of you. No good can come from feeling angry.

The easiest way to diffuse anger can also be the most difficult thing to do—decide. You have spent a long time building up your case to remain angry.

There might even be years of piling hurtful evidence in the arsenal. Anger is based on pride and a need to be right in order to have self-worth. All this "proof," if you will, makes it difficult to turn your thought process around, but it can be done.

Most of us have been taught that in order to solve a problem, we need to focus on the problem and look for solutions; but what if you focused on the solution instead? If the solution is the outcome you desire, your mind will try to find a way to achieve it. Ask yourself this question: "What is it that I want?"

Do you want to be more understanding, thinner, have more money? It is a simple question, one that deserves some sincere consideration. When you can figure out the outcome you desire of a situation, that outcome becomes your goal. It is exciting to focus on what you want, much more than thinking about solving a problem. When you know what the desired outcome is, it becomes easier to figure out how to get there; and when you figure out how to get there, the steps fall into place naturally. This will subdue those angry feelings you have.

There is one good thing that is present in anger, and that is the passion you feel. Granted, it is negative, but imagine how you would feel if you separated the passion from the anger and turn it into compassion? Can't you feel the peaceful

> *Don't hold to anger, hurt, or pain. They steal your energy and keep you from love.*
> —Leo Buscaglia

change within just by considering this process? When you focus on turning hate into love, you are acknowledging that you are ready to receive a gift from God. It is so much more fulfilling to live with love in your heart rather than hatred and anger.

I heard a story the other day about a meeting between United States President Reagan and the first president of the former Soviet Union, Mikhail Gorbachev, trying to figure out how to solve the Cold War. As we all know, the

East and West have very different philosophies about how their countries are run. Both leaders were convinced that his way was the better way of life. As the men sat there attempting to convince each other of his point of view, the conversation level became more intense and started spiraling as clouds do at the inception of a tornado.

President Reagan talked of free trade and freedom of speech, while President Gorbachev pointed out the benefits of communism. The conversation got louder and louder and turned into a heated argument, with each of them reaching high levels of anger. Then, all of the sudden, President Reagan got up and began to walk toward the door. President Gorbachev was stunned. Just at that moment, Reagan turned around with a big smile on his face and said, "Let's start over. Hi, my name is Ron."

Thus began the candid discussion of two of the world's most powerful leaders to end the Cold War. At that instant, the beliefs that the other represented evil and was the enemy dissolved into seeing each other as human beings. When that happens, possibilities open up and they both were able to see there could be a solution.

If President Reagan would have stormed out of the room in anger, the death of the meeting would have been the result rather than a continuance of the conversation.

Overcoming anger is one of the most life-enforcing feats one can accomplish. Diffuse your anger and you will experience a wonderful new world.

Fear

Fear

Whoa! Tough subject to approach when you are in a position and place that reeks of fear and hatred. In order to overcome fear, you must first define it, and then face it.

Let's put a definition on it. Fear is an emotion, which is something you are in control of. It does not define you unless you allow it to. Fear is a distressing emotion aroused by impending danger, evil, pain, and so on, whether the threat is real or imagined.

Another definition of fear is having reverential awe, such as for God.

Throughout our lifetimes, we have been in situations with which we are unfamiliar. Because it is human nature to be cautious of unknown things, we have a built-in fear of that which is unfamiliar. To cope with our situation, we reference our past experiences and their outcomes to guide us through this uncharted territory. This can be a good choice if our experiences have led us to improve who we are in this lifetime. Such enhancing experiences mean growth and choosing life.

However, if instead, we choose to reference an experience that either puts off dealing with the problem or distorts the solution to fit areas that make us comfortable, we become indecisive. The lack of choosing to face the issue will make it bigger and harder to solve, thus creating more fear. Until the fear is defined with truth, it cannot be alleviated because we cannot get rid of something if we don't know what it is.

So, step up and get in fear's face, dig deep and ask the tough questions of yourself and be honest. Turn your thoughts away from "what will people think? What if I fail? What if the answer is no? What if..., what if? Write down your thoughts and be honest with yourself. Look in the mirror and tell yourself what it is no matter how painful it is, so you can move on.

So there it is, in black and white or reflecting back at you from the mirror: THE FEAR. When you stare fear in the face, a tiny little glimmer of hope will begin to surface, and out of that tiny hope, courage shows up as well. Recognizing and acknowledging the fear is the first step toward eliminating fear.

Now focus on the glimmer of hope that is trying to make its way to the front. Does it become larger as you focus on it? Is it becoming lighter? Do you feel less pressure or more pressure? Do you feel stronger or weaker? When you begin to notice each change

> *One of the things I learned the hard way was that it doesn't pay to get discouraged. Keeping busy and making optimism a way of life can restore your faith in yourself.*
> —Lucille Ball

that occurs as you focus on the *hope*fulness of the situation rather than the *fear*fulness, the mind and body will acknowledge this great feeling and make it part of who you are and a change occurs. When this process is repeated over and over, it builds the courage to respond to the lesson in a positive way rather than allowing you to drown in the fear.

The second step to overcoming a fear requires evaluating the aspects of your fear. What is the reward for overcoming this fear? What can you gain? What happens if you do nothing to overcome this fear? What is that reward? Will you feel comfort by proving that you are justified to be afraid because you have always felt that way in the past? Will you feel stronger or weaker if you hold on to your fear? Do you feel more or less pressure? Notice how holding on to the fear makes you feel.

Compare the two feelings—fear and hope—and choose the belief that will improve your current state and focus on it. By doing this, you are leveraging the ability to eliminate the fearful emotion you are experiencing. This is creating your own very individual "why." So now you have named your fear and why you would like to get rid of it.

The next step becomes much easier now that you have created the motivation to overcome fear. Now it is time to put into action the "how" to eliminate this nasty, emotional fear. This is another evaluation step that lets you seek out the various alternatives and how they will impact changing the fearful emotion and the outcome you desire by eliminating that fear. Give yourself permission to get a little crazy here and come up with as many solutions as you like. The sky's the limit. Your possible solutions can be outrageous, silly, or whatever you can come up with.

For example, if you are trying to figure out how to eliminate the fear of darkness, visualize sitting in the dark. Allow yourself to feel the fear of all that could possibly happen to you. Each time you feel that fear, create a means to overcome it. Turn it into a cartoon where Donald Duck is sitting in the dark with his eyes wide open and dark all around him, when suddenly, he has an idea and the light bulb above his head lights up.

For you, it might be as simple as standing up and turning on a light switch, or opening a curtain, or maybe when you stand up and feel your strength, the darkness becomes lighter. This activity minimizes the value of the fear you are trying to overcome and may help lead you to the conclusion that the fear you perceived to be so big or real was just an incorrect belief that needed attention. You can now get back on the right path because your footing is now on solid ground, one that has solutions to the uneasy emotion of fear.

Moses

One of the most impactful examples of fear and overcoming it is straight out of the Bible in the story of Moses and the role given to him by God himself. Moses was born a Hebrew and just before his birth, the Pharaoh, ruler of Egypt, issued an order, out of the fear that the Israelites would soon outnumber the Egyptians, to throw all the newborn boys into the Nile River. Fearing that her newborn baby would be discovered, Moses' mother devised a waterproof basket in which she placed Moses in so he could float down the Nile. Ultimately, the Pharaoh's daughter found the infant in the basket. Just like a child finding a puppy, she brought him home to her father and asked if she could keep him.

> Anything I've ever done that ultimately was worthwhile ultimately scared me to death.
> —Betty Bender

Moses grew up in the house of Egypt. One day, he encountered an Egyptian slave master beating a Hebrew slave. Outraged at the injustice, Moses kills the slave master and buries him in the desert. Moses did not know that anyone had seen him do this. When it was apparent that there had been witnesses, the news of the murder got back to the Pharaoh. Moses fearfully fled into the desert to avoid punishment. There he became a shepherd, married, and had a son.

As time passed, the ruler of Egypt died and God saw the misery of his chosen people, the Hebrews, under the suppression of the Egyptians. This is when God chose Moses to save them. He did not choose a powerful, eloquently spoken orator, He chose Moses—a murderer, a coward, and more importantly, a Jew who had killed an Egyptian. God spoke to Moses through the burning bush to tell him of His plan.

Can you imagine the kind of fear Moses felt when God first approached him? It was different than the fear of any person in the physical world and God assured Moses He would be with him and that Moses should have faith. Thus began the long struggle of the Hebrew population to become free from Egyptian oppression. Moses did have faith and trusted God to lead them to the Promised Land. Moses' courage to overcome his fear of inadequacies was because he had faith in God.

Whether or not you believe in God, Buddha, Allah or whatever superhuman force that governs your world, the key to remember is the faith that guides you in your life will accompany you on your path to overcoming fear and choosing life.

If you remember from the chapter on Confinement, Jaycee Dugard grew up learning to fear as a way of life to the same extent I am sure you might have as well. When she was kidnapped at age eleven, her life changed drastically from one of knowing what to expect to a life of ultimate uncertainty. The uncertainly she faced each day ironically became her comfort that helped her keep her sanity, something to hang onto and that she could count on. She learned to count on fear; it was not only the enemy, but also her comfort because she knew it would be there day after day. Her captors had turned her into a fearful being and made her totally reliant on them for her existence.

After years in captivity, she became so dependent that the physical walls of confinement were no longer necessary because stronger walls of confinement had been constructed in her mind. By the time Stacy was freed from her physical confinement, she found that she was unable to free herself from the mental prison she had constructed during the years of captivity. From the day of her release to this present day, she continues to work to rid herself of the fear in her life.

Jaycee Dugard has never given in to accepting a life of fear. She seeks answers to disable the crippling, learned fear that inhabited her soul for so many years.

Eliminating fear is not something that you can do overnight, but you can consciously decide to begin the process. Do the inner reflection and ask your supreme power for help. You do not have to do this alone. Every successful thought you have will bring a little window of hope to you and that window of hope will make you feel life. When you feel this life, enjoy that feeling, and recognize it as your right to feel good. That peace you feel is the ultimate outcome we all deserve to experience. Make this your motivation to continue the work on eliminating fear in your life.

Overcoming fear takes time. Be patient with yourself. Hang onto the hope of peace. Do the work and that peace will come.

The Shame Game

The Shame Game

Shame is a negative emotion that combines feelings of dishonor, unworthiness, and embarrassment. Everyone knows that shame is a negative feeling. There are things we do or say that make us feel ashamed at one time or another.

Two questions come to mind here. The first is *why do we feel ashamed*? In our life's journey, we experience situations that present us with decisions that need to be made and results that come from those decisions. Then our brain puts in its two cents and weighs all the past decisions we have made to determine if the most current decision falls in line with the majority of choices we have made in the past. When the current outcome falls outside the brain's evaluation of what is deemed acceptable and right, a feeling of shame can enter because our choice does not coincide with what the experiences have meant previously.

Our belief systems have taken many years to develop and allow us to come to the conclusions the brain arrives at. These beliefs didn't happen overnight or without influence. Each choice made is influenced by the all-inclusive mass of decisions we have compiled to date.

As an example, let's take two friends and co-workers, Tom and Bill. Bill has discovered a great idea to solve a problem that everyone has struggled to answer. He is excited that he has a solution and shares it with Tom, but for one reason or another, he cannot present the idea to his superior until tomorrow. When Tom hears Bill's idea, he becomes excited as well and decides to present the idea immediately to the superiors who can facilitate it, but instead of presenting it as Bill's idea, Tom takes the credit. The idea gets a lot of attention and becomes a huge success, which results in countless praise and accolades.

The next day, he sees Bill, who is still excited about his idea and perplexed that Tom is less than enthusiastic about his excitement. The less-than-enthusiastic feeling Tom has is called shame, for his action of "stealing" Bill's idea and presenting it as his own, was less than honorable behavior.

When we make choices that dishonor who we are and are outside what is acceptable to our belief system, then shame and guilt will flood our being. The embarrassment of the actions taken has created a negative emotional environment between Tom and Bill. Not a very warm and fuzzy feeling.

The second question that shame brings to mind is: *"How does it impact us?"* Being one of the negative emotions, we all know that shame will not promote growth or life in a human experience. Just as a knife cuts through a piece of meat and divides it in two, shame can cut us off from positive events that could have happened had you made better choices. Now what faces us is living with the negative choices, rather than growing with good and wholesome decisions leading us positively in life's journey. Shame and guilt can be devastating to the development of confidence in a person, but they can be overcome.

Let's continue with the example of the two friends, Bill and Tom. The uncomfortable situation created by Tom's shameful activity can be repaired. It is apparent that Bill has no idea that Tom deceived him by presenting Bill's idea as his own, so if Tom can muster up the courage to tell Bill what he did, it will be painful and uncomfortable in the present. The outcome could result in a rift in the relationship or forgiveness if Tom truly rectifies his actions. This would be embarrassing, but ultimately the right thing to do. To completely correct the mistrust that was created, the action must be carried out fully, which would require an apology to Bill and a confession of who truly deserved the credit to the higher ups. While such action could possibly salvage the relationship with Bill, it might also damage Tom's credibility with the higher ups.

If Tom does not tell Bill what he did and Bill finds out on his own, it will be painful and the outcome could result in a rift in the relationship. Bill will be hurt and angry with Tom. The fact that Tom did not confess the wrongdoing to him will likely lead Bill to believe that Tom has little or no regard for his feelings.

> *A man is not hurt by so much by what happens, as by his opinion of what happens.*
> —Michel de Montaigne

Both solutions are difficult choices. It is up to each individual to choose the one that will cause the least pain. If you think about it, there are really only two choices that motivate us to make decisions in life: to avoid pain or gain pleasure.

When Tom presented Bill's idea as his own and received the praise and accolades, he received pleasure in the short term. Because that pleasure was not aligned with Tom's inner belief system of right and wrong, it was a fleeting moment that turned into an outcome where he was faced with two painful solutions.

When shame and guilt are internalized and never dealt with honestly, they cripple development in a positive direction. There are times when being ashamed of something is an indirect action of somebody else and not the result of a personal action. A good example of that would be growing up in an environment of poverty and crime with the negative influence of peers.

Because there are no examples of what is right or just, one would tend to believe that the behavior and actions of one's peers are the truth of how life is supposed to be for them: "I don't need an education and it is cool to drop out of school," "I am poor and always will be," "It's OK to take what belongs to others," "Nice things are for the rich, not me." Those messages can go on and on. When these beliefs become your beliefs and are taken into the world outside the comfort of the poverty in which you live, it becomes uncomfortable and the feeling of shame can come over you.

There is a movie called *The Blind Side* that tells of a young man born in a very impoverished environment. His mother is a drug addict and alcoholic who isn't sure who his father is. They live in rundown rooms or sometimes homeless. Michael is often put into foster care. He is faced with the pressure of joining gangs and committing to a life of crime. The young man is large and physically strong, but is broken and scared inside.

At the opposite end of the spectrum is an upper-middle-class family, the Tuohys, who live in the more affluent part of town. The mother notices Michael walking the streets late at night with a bag in hand and no coat, though it is the middle of winter. She approaches the young man to see why he has no coat. She has also heard from her own children that Michael does not eat anything in the lunchroom at school.

After several attempts to help this young man, he finally accepts their offer to come stay at the Tuohy's home. As the story progresses, he learns a new way of life, graduates from high school, and goes on to college on a football scholarship. As the story ends, Michael Ohon ends up being drafted by the Baltimore Ravens to play left tackle on the professional league team.

Had Michael not faced his fears of overcoming his unfortunate background, none of this would have happened. He learned that he was not his past and the circumstances that were his past experience did not define him, unless he let it. Michael's shame was not because of his actions, but came from the actions of his environment and peers. His belief was that he was worth less than the Tuohy's, but when his pain became great enough, he was ready to make a change in his belief system.

Shedding shame will free you from the imaginary shackles that have been placed around your life. Let go of the guilt and shame and live your life as a new person. Know that everything is possible if you want it deeply enough. Confront the shame and guilt, and do the work necessary to overcome those negative attributes so you can move in a new direction with confidence. By telling you to do the work, I am not saying to rationalize it, but to strip away the layers of opinions and beliefs that have been covering this issue that shames you to see what is really the truth of the matter.

> *The only thing that stands between a man and what he wants from life is often merely the will to try it and the faith to believe that it is possible.*
> —Richard M. Devos

Ask yourself, "Is this shame something I created, or is this shame a product of an atmosphere I do not control?" Once you know what it is you need to change, the solution will be easier to come by.

Let's go back to Bill and Tom. Tom created the shame he experiences by choosing the short-term pleasurable feeling he attained from being commended for Bill's idea. He must take responsibility for his actions and realize that he did something that was in conflict with his moral values. He must own up to his actions.

Feeling this uncomfortable truth about yourself creates a desire to change the feeling to a good one, which creates motivation to change the outcome. The outcome then becomes one that will be pleasing. Let's say Tom wants to feel joy for Bill's success. Tom now knows how he wants to feel; he just needs to map out the plan of how to get there. Once you know what it is you need to change, the solution will become easier to figure out.

In Michael's story, leaving his former life was very difficult for him. As horrendous as his former impoverished lifestyle was, it gave him a level of comfort because it was familiar. What he faced was the fact that if he wanted his life to change for the better, he would be leaving behind the comfort of the peer group he had known, as well as the not-so-desirable circumstances in which he was raised. It may sound like a no brainer, but choosing an unknown fate can be a very daunting decision.

Both these stories are meant to inspire and help you overcome whatever it is that shames you. It takes courage to face the flaws we develop throughout our lives, but when we can develop the courage to look at the truth of our shame, it usually isn't as bad as we have made it out to be. Each day, we wake up with a new opportunity to do it right, so as Nike puts it—*JUST DO IT!*

Forgiveness

Forgiveness

When you choose to forgive someone, you are releasing one of the most damaging, self-inflicted powers that exists—anger.

Forgiveness is the act of pardoning another for a mistake or wrongdoing. This is not an easy thing to do because it is not our nature as human beings to release a perceived or physical injury. Our nature is to protect the character we have developed by our choices made throughout our lives. Defending our side of the story does not lead to growth; it leads to death, for lack of a better word. Hanging onto anger or hurt can end any possibilities of future relationship with the offending person. Harboring such thoughts and feelings can lead to unhealthy thoughts and physical ailments if left to fester inside us.

By choosing forgiveness, we can experience new life, inner peace, and move forward. This is what God intends for us, and by making this choice, we are delivering a positive message that enhances our human experience here on earth. What a powerful thing to do! We all have the capacity to make this happen.

We may consciously make a decision to forgive someone, but maybe the heart is not ready to follow, or vice versa. What are the options to get to the point of wholeheartedly forgiving someone? Maybe a person needs time to heal. When someone you love dies, the period following that person's death is for grieving or processing the loss and finding the peace that we need to arise out of the loss of their physical presence. The same can be said for the period leading up to forgiveness.

Another way to help us reach the point of forgiveness is to enlist the aid of a trusted advisor, spiritual leader, or even a friend you trust. Sometimes we cannot objectively evaluate the situation because our emotional selves are blocking the path to the answer we need that will allow us to forgive. By receiving objective input, our emotional blocks can be changed to this new perspective and the path can become clear, allowing forgiveness to flow freely from both our consciousness and heart. When your heart and mind are in unison, then true forgiveness can happen.

Mary Johnson

In Minnesota in 1993, a man named Oshea Israel murdered a nineteen-year-old boy named Laramiun Lamont Byrd. Oshea took the boy's life by shooting him numerous times and leaving his lifeless body outside a local hospital. This action stripped his mother of a future with her son, as well as the possibility of grandchildren, and sent her into a decade of feeling anger and hatred toward her son's murderer.

Israel was convicted of the crime and sent to prison to deal with the repercussions of his actions. Mrs. Byrd (Mary) Johnson, Laramiun's mother, felt justice had been served by caging the animal who had taken her son's life. But it still did not make her feel the peace she so desperately wanted inside. Each day that Mary focused on the "justice" that had been served and the "righteousness" the legal system had delivered, she was reinforcing her anger toward her son's murderer. She started paying attention to the little voice that kept telling her that she needed to face the inner despair and allow forgiveness not only toward Israel, but for herself as well. Her anger prevented her from living her life.

When you release the wrongdoer from the wrong, you cut a malignant tumor out of your inner life. You set a prisoner free, but you discover that the real prisoner was yourself.
—Lewis B. Smedes

After seventeen years in prison, Oshea Israel was released, at which time Mrs. Johnson decided it was time to face the man and this fierce hurt that she had built up over those years. As their eyes met, Mary Johnson fell to her knees and began to sob. She physically could feel all the hurt and anger leave her body as she totally and unequivocally forgave Oshea Israel for murdering her son.

That moment in time was not only a miracle for Mary, but for Oshea as well. Her powerful act of forgiveness birthed an overwhelming feeling of gratitude for Israel. Out of this act of hatred came a beautiful story of love and forgiveness. Mary and Oshea found a life-enforcing bond that they both feel was created by God's guidance.

Forgive the Beast

The next story I am about to tell you is quite personal, for it is my own story of how I struggled with forgiveness. On a cold winter day in 2007, I sat in a chair with my hot cup of coffee, contemplating why I had made such bad decisions with regard to the men I allowed in my life. Each of the three relationships I had chosen to be in were abusive in their own ways. In my marriage, I allowed physical abuse; in the second relationship, I allowed infidelity, and most recently, I tolerated mental abuse.

As I watched the snow blowing outside my window, I could see the parallel of the reckless relationship decisions I had made and the snow that was blown wherever the gales took it. The question of "why" had been nagging at me since the end of the most recent disaster of a relationship and it was not going away. Just like a toothache that continues to throb and erode, the annoying "why" question was becoming an abscess, spreading the poison and spoiling who I was meant to be.

I began journaling. You could say that was the beginning of my quest to express myself through writing. The one thing about sitting down to intentionally put your thoughts in writing is that it forces you to ask questions of yourself. The thing that I wasn't prepared for was the answer.

The painful truth came flooding back as if the dam burst open. I had totally blocked out the memory of being molested as a child for most of my life and now, here it was, in my face to be dealt with fifty years later. At age eight, I was repeatedly molested by the neighbor boy ten years my senior while he was babysitting me. He would bring me up to his attic bedroom and tell me that after we played his game, he would play any game that I wanted to play. I remember the dread and fear I felt when I knew I would have to go over to that house, I knew it was wrong, but the neighbor boy told me that if I mentioned anything to my parents, I would be in trouble, so I kept the shameful truth tucked away to fester for years and years.

I remember trying to tell my parents and they must have known that something was not right because eventually, the boy's babysitting days were over. His sick actions were never addressed nor did my parents ever acknowledge that the molestations happened. His parents remained unaware that their son had done anything wrong.

I was stunned that I could actually block the entire experience out of my memory for most of my life. I could feel the rage brewing up inside about the tremendous impact these suppressed childhood memories had had on my life. The explosion of anger I felt would dwarf anything a volcano could spew. I was shocked when I looked back on all the years I unconsciously made poor relational choices. What was I to do with this memory? How do I overcome the anger toward the neighbor boy, my parents, or even God for allowing this to happen?

> *Holding on to anger is like grasping a hot coal with the intent of throwing it at someone else; you are the one who gets burned.*
> —Buddha

The answer might have been simple— *forgive*— but the act of forgiving was not that easy.

I went over the gruesome details again and again to try to find the answer about why that had happened to me. I cried and felt sorry for myself, but that didn't help. Blaming my parents for not helping me handle my grief didn't help either; they loved me and did the best they knew how to keep me safe.

I tried to blame God for allowing the abuse to happen to me, but came to the realization that God had not done it to me—a mortal boy had. The most logical person to blame for my anger was the boy, but that didn't help either. I learned from my parents that he had died some time ago, so confronting him was not an option.

In time, God led me to the realization that the only thing that would allow me to move on was to accept that it happened and let the anger go—forgive the neighbor boy. No one in this earthly world is perfect. We all have our flaws and sitting in judgment of those flaws is not my job—it is God's.

That deep, dark secret is no longer my shame. I no longer carry that burden. I have forgiven. Now I think of this event in another way—one that led me to writing this book for you.

Choosing to forgive is a huge step toward healing. It is an act that will change your entire life the moment you decide to forgive someone for a wrong. You are letting go of the past and creating a new life for not only yourself, but for many others as well. When you make the conscious change from anger and resentment and become a compassionate, forgiving person, the energy around you changes. What you attract in your life becomes positive. Inside, you no longer feel the constriction of anger, but begin to feel the joy of peace.

It may take some time to fully forgive. I still have times when I struggle with releasing the anger and hurt. No one said life was going to be easy. In fact, life's most meaningful experiences are the result of overcoming difficulties. These can be your "AHA" moments. If you have a slight relapse, it's OK. Be forgiving to yourself. Maybe the next attempt will give you the peace you are looking for. That is the beauty of life: God always gives you another chance. If you follow His lead, you are on the right track.

Judgment

Judgment

Whether you find yourself confined within a prison that has physical walls or a prison that has been mentally created, it is because a judgment has been made. If you are incarcerated and serving time in prison, let's take a look at the judgment that put you where you are today. Incarceration stops an individual from continuing activity that has been declared by society to be unacceptable, and therefore protects society from further harm by that individual, as well as protecting the individual from doing more harm to himself.

Legal systems are set up to serve and protect the people in this world. The law was created to reflect the rights created by our forefathers in the Constitution and ultimately from the Ten Commandments issued by God, the supreme Judge. Being judged by the authorities of the law for an act against the law of the land is for the protection of the majority.

Many inmates say that they have been judged unfairly and are innocent of the crime of which they were accused or that they are "victims" of society. That may be true, but such victims make the decision to continue with the life choices of their peers, knowing they were wrong choices rather than forge a new way of life that leads them toward independence of poor decisions. It is easier to follow the group of peers who have already accepted a life of crime than to walk away and forge a new lifestyle that leads to a righteous one. It is unfamiliar territory and can be quite intimidating because this means closing a door on one lifestyle and standing at the threshold of a new one.

> *If you keep doing what you've always done, you will keep getting what you've always got.*
> —Peter Francisco

Did you ever think that you are being saved from something that could be more detrimental to you than the crime for which you were convicted? A good example would be a teen who began using marijuana in high school just to fit in with his peers. In the beginning, it was fun to join in because everyone was doing it so the teen felt justified in continuing to use the illegal drug. Then maybe a friend suggested trying something a little different to give the teen another kind of feeling, a little crack. It led the teen into a whole new arena in the drug world. The teen knows that using drugs is wrong, but again, he justifies it with the "everyone else is doing it" excuse. The teen knows deep inside that not everyone else is doing it, but the peers he associates with are, and that is all that matters to him.

The teen likes how he feels from doing a little crack, but the stuff is expensive, so he has to find a way to earn enough money to pay for it. He starts selling the drug, begins making a bunch of money, and gets to do all the crack he wants. Now he is addicted to it and out of control. All that matters is getting the drug, not who he swindles, who he steps on, who he cheats, who he kills. All that matters is getting the drug.

> The best way to escape from a problem is to solve it.
> —Anonymous

One day, the teen gets busted and put in jail. This may be God's way of intervening to save his life, freeing him from addiction and allowing the teen the time find his way back to Him.

It can be hard to face the truth. Often, we will choose to pretend that the truth is not the truth, but in reality, facing the truth is what frees us.

Creating new behavior involves personal courage and will change our lives for the better. It can also displease the group of victims in your current environment. Doing the right thing is not an easy task, but the great thing about it is that it is worth each and every good choice we make.

When we change our heart, we can change our life. Each day, we are given a new opportunity to start fresh, to think new thoughts, to choose a new direction. When this happens, we are beginning a new life, one that inspires us to be better people.

Stand up for yourself and be strong against the temptation of going along with the crowd, unless the crowd represents what you want from your life—to remain a victim of society. You be the judge, take control of your future by making the most of your present.

Everyone struggles with judgment. Our belief system has been formed from all the experiences we have had in our lives, which makes each and every one of us a unique piece of art in God's gallery. That being said, you can see why God does not leave it up to us to make judgments on our own, because our views of what is right or wrong or good or bad will vary, depending upon our beliefs. In order to help us make sound decisions, God gave us his laws for us to abide by: the Ten Commandments.

THE TEN COMMANDMENTS

1. I am the Lord thy God.
2. Thou shalt have no other gods before me.
3. Thou shalt not swear falsely by the name of the Lord.
4. Remember the Sabbath Day and keep it holy.
5. Honor thy father and mother.
6. Thou shalt not kill.
7. Thou shalt not commit adultery.
8. Thou shalt not steal.
9. Thou shalt not bear false witness against thy neighbor.
10. Thou shalt not covet thy neighbor's wife (goods).

Let's face it, we as human beings are flawed and have at one time or another broken one or more of the Command-ments, maybe even all of them. We all know that stealing is wrong, but still it is

tempting to do so, either out of despera-
tion or greed. Deep inside, we feel the
twinge of guilt (self-judgment) when we
take something that does not belong to
us and in that moment, are convicting
ourselves.

The problem arises when we begin to
rationalize our actions so we can free
ourselves of the self-conviction. This is
altering the "do not steal" commandment
to fit our individual set of circumstances.
When we do that, we are no longer
obeying the law of God, we are creating a
law that serves us. If humanity were to
exist without a system to enforce the law,
there would be complete and utter chaos
with rebellion and self-judgments running rampant. The world needs a set of
guidelines by which to operate so we can
live in a safe and healthy environment.

If you choose to live outside the law,
there are consequences you must face. It
is really very simple if you look at it this
way.

One of the most difficult aspects to
face when we are being judged is to be
truthful with ourselves about our partici-

pation in the act for which we are facing judgment. When we can do that, God can forgive us because we honor Him by acknowledging that we know His law is good and that our actions were not in accordance with His law.

The legal systems that exist on our planet are an extension of His will to be done "here on earth as it is in heaven." These laws are not perfect because human beings are not perfect, but it is necessary to have an orderly plan by which our society can live. There are many interpretations of justice in our world that come from different religions and cultures, but they all have the same common bond and that is to keep peace.

When we can own up to our conviction and confess our sin (to God, not the warden), then forgiveness can happen for us. Will the consequences go away? Probably not, nor should they. The punishment was issued to you for your own good and allows time for you to realize your mistakes so you can begin with a clear conscience in a new direction, one that is pleasing and acceptable to not only God, but society as well.

So what if you are judged and being confined for an act of which you are not guilty? No, it isn't fair, not by the interpretation of the law that we live by on earth. Sometimes the lot you have been given in life is unjust in your eyes, but may be a test of your faith from above.

> When you have something to prove, there's nothing better than a challenge.
> —Terry Bradshaw

In the Old Testament, Joseph was unjustly accused and thrown into prison by the Pharaoh of Egypt. The Pharaoh's wife had told her husband that Joseph had made advances on her, when in fact that had never happened. Joseph served Pharaoh with the honor and respect that was given to him and did not dishonor the Pharaoh's wife. Nevertheless, Pharaoh threw him in prison for a crime he did not commit.

So what did Joseph do? He remained faithful to his Lord and found favor with the prison warden. He became so trusted by the warden that all prison issues were no longer a concern to him, Joseph did the good works he was entrusted with. Eventually the news of his good works reached the Pharaoh and Joseph was returned to a high position in Egypt, the second in command next to the Pharaoh.

The message here is to do the best you can with every situation you have been given and you will be rewarded by the Universe with the satisfaction that you did your best. When positive energy is put into the world, it flows back to you, just as a breath does when you expel it.

Being convicted of murder results in serious punishment and if you are inno-cent of that crime, how can you maintain a righteous attitude without feeling bitter? It is not an easy thing to do and life can be unjust, but it is what you do with your situation that determines the state of your soul. If you choose to re-main bitter and angry about the unjust conviction, then that is the life you will have—one filled with anger. If you choose to accept that which you cannot change and do the best you can about your current situation, then life will be more peaceful because you internally accept that you are not in control of what is happening to you, God is. When you give your problems up and over to Him, He will be there for you and His peace will be yours.

By the understanding of justice that we have in this world, a false conviction is very unfair, but the faith in God to help you handle it will go a lot further than holding on to anger.

The next time you think of judging someone, try to remember that the result is life-enforcing (love) or life-ending (death) in your relationship with that person. Make sure that you use the good judgment that God has given us to serve Him.

Proud to be Humble

Proud to be Humble

Being proud of yourself can be either a good thing or a bad thing. It depends upon the reason you are experiencing it. The definition of pride is a high or inordinate opinion of one's importance; a superiority of sorts. From the experiences in my life, I had always interpreted pride to be a good attribute, but my opinion had expanded over the years. I realize now that pride is a complex emotion that can take on different meanings.

When she was a young girl, a woman had a falling out with her mother over something hurtful her mother said to her. This is how the rift in their relationship initially started. As years went by, the silence grew and the resentment that came from the incident grew as well, kind of the snowball effect. During this period of time, the daughter had gotten married, had a child and been divorced— all without any communication with her mother. The mother tried several times to talk with her daughter, who did not respond to her attempts. The daughter felt that she was right in her evaluation of the incident and let her pride get in the way of not only having a relationship with her mother, but also denying her husband and daughter the possibility of ever knowing her grandmother. In addition, she also eliminated relationships with her sister (aunt), father (grandfather) and several friends over time because her need to be right outweighed her need for relationship with them.

> You can't get much done in life if you only work on the days when you feel good.
> —Jerry West

Pride can be a very costly state of being if you let it consume you as this woman did. Her need to avoid pain in the relationship arena was greater than her need to get pleasure in relationships.

It can be hard to humble yourself and admit you might be wrong, or that you forgive someone, but if you hold on to that resentment for no other reason than your self-importance of being right, it can cost you dearly. Let down your defenses and turn the other cheek, make amends and be humble. The irony is that once you have humbled yourself, you will feel a new kind of pride in knowing you have made someone feel worthy at the expense of giving up your own need to be right. The act of being humble is one of life's unsung attributes, which rarely gets the accolades it so richly deserves. The definition of humble as I see it is not feeling pride in one's self, and giving credit to those who participated in your success, the act of being unpretentious; not arrogant.

One of the best examples of a humble person is Lou Gehrig, an attitude which ironically led to his becoming "The Pride of the Yankees." He was born in 1903 to

German immigrants who did whatever it took to put food on the table. Being the only child out of four to survive, his parents were determined to get him a good education, no matter what it took to do so. Lou did make his way into college on a football scholarship, but was discovered to have superior talent in baseball.

> *The Babe is one fellow, and I'm another and I could never be exactly like him. I don't try. I just go on as I am in my own right.*
> —Lou Gehrig

Lou Gehrig became a Yankee during the glory days of Babe Ruth and was always lost in the Babe's shadow. It never bothered Lou; he just wanted to do the best he could and that he did. Everyone knew him as a genuinely nice guy who unselfishly devoted himself to perfecting his talent for the team. His skills excelled and he was rewarded with honor after honor. He had some physical health issues often playing with pain and a broken thumb or sprained body part, but never complained, thereby earning the nickname "the Iron Horse."

In 1938, it was becoming apparent that his skills were deteriorating and his physical health was the cause. After a great deal of observation at the Mayo Clinic, it was determined that he had a degenerative disease called ALS, amyotrophic lateral sclerosis—later to be referred to as Lou Gehrig Disease.

Lou's baseball days were over and life ahead would be very challenging. It was suggested that a day be named to honor Lou Gehrig and all he had done for the sport of baseball, and on July 4, 1939, he was given that honor. His speech was humble, giving thanks to the fans, his team, coaches and family for all the blessings he had in life calling himself one of the luckiest men on earth. Everyone loved Lou Gehrig because of his humility. Two years later, he died. His unselfish demeanor gained him the respect of all he came in contact with.

By being humble, you have much more to gain than if you are prideful. When you give yourself the accolades, it doesn't feel the same as when someone else notices your talent and credits you. Feeling joy from an accomplishment done well is the state desired, not pointing out your accomplishment to others and indicating superiority. Whether you acknowledge it or not, you did not achieve the success all by yourself; there were others in your life that contributed along the way. It could be a coach, a lesson you learned, a teacher or a friend; give credit to those who helped and supported you—it's a much more gracious path to follow.

Being humble, as in Lou Gehrig's story, can stir admiration of that person from others and almost always does. It is good to honor others with the good feeling that comes from recognizing their exemplary actions.

For instance, you can be proud of your children and give them the credit, rather than you claiming credit for their behavior. Their behavior is a result of decisions and choices they have made. You may have influenced them as a parent in their formative years and you can feel joy about that; but taking away the accomplishment they so rightly deserve and claiming it for yourself is not an act that will bring you honor.

Pride and humility dance together—when humility takes the lead, it stirs pride and respect from others. When pride takes the lead, being humbled is sure to follow. The Bible has over 95 scriptures on the virtue of being humble to teach us that we should always honor others before ourselves.

Do you remember the story of the *Emperor's New Clothes*? Two con artists entered town and pretended to be weavers because they knew the Emperor had an obsession for fine clothing. They let the word be spread that there were no finer weavers in the land. When the news got back to the Emperor, he summoned them to the castle to weave him a superior set of clothes. They set up the looms and were given the finest of silks and gold thread, which they pocketed. The swindlers demanded complete privacy to perform their miraculous creation of the finest clothes in the land. They burned candle after candle and ran the loom day and night weaving clothes so fine they were invisible. Non-existent really.

When the king sent in his trusted advisors to check on the progress, they saw nothing; but were too proud to admit that they saw nothing, so they went back to the Emperor and told him of their beauty. The weavers were finishing up the scam of a project and the Emperor could hardly wait to try on these fine clothes and show them to his kingdom. He entered the room only to find the two weavers standing there holding nothing. Since his trusted advisors had reported the beauty and fine craftsmanship of the clothing, he could hardly admit that he could not see them, so he raved of their beauty and the swindle of the scam artists continued.

As the weavers helped him into his non-existent clothes, the advisors embellished the charade by feigning approval of the superior quality the clothes possessed. When the king paraded through the streets of his kingdom in his underwear, a little girl pointed her finger and said, "Look, Mommy, the Emperor has no clothes on." The crowd began to laugh and agreed that the king was in his underwear. The Emperor was beginning to see that the crowd was right, but could not agree because then they would know he was a fool, so he continued with the charade. His pride got in the way of admitting the truth.

> *I made it this far, a fool with my foolish pride. Look at me, what do you see? A fool and his foolish pride.*
> —Young Jeezy

How often does this happen in real life? By the king's non-admission of knowing the truth that he had been fooled, he separated himself from his kingdom.

The story ends here and we do not know what happens to the king after his embarrassing display of his "new clothes," but let's create some possibilities. Do you think it is possible that the subjects in his kingdom may begin to doubt his judgment? I know if I were one of them, I would feel that way; and in feeling that way, wouldn't it seem logical that the future of his leadership was in jeopardy? With the separation he created by continuing the ruse, he distanced himself from a good portion of the people, which could generate turmoil and create unrest.

Would it not have been better to humble himself to praise his kingdom (feel pride in them) for their keen observation in recognizing the truth? In doing so, he would be giving praise to them and as a result, they would feel love and respect for him. When you have the respect of someone, the mistakes you may make along the way are more easily forgiven.

Feeling pride for others is an honorable emotion. Humble yourself; because the credit is never all yours. Without the guidance from the Universe, God, Buddha, or whatever else you might believe it, we cannot achieve anything. If you give credit where credit is really due and thank your power of being, you will experience the joy that is intended for you.

Never Too Old

Never Too Old

Throughout our lifetimes, all of our experiences shape who we are at this present moment. The input from television, books, advertisements, other people's opinions, and numerous other sources can change our beliefs from those that empower to those that disempower.

When the disempowering beliefs outnumber those that empower us and expand who we are, the world at our disposal becomes a little smaller, more confining. After years and years of negative input, the tendency is to believe what is heard as truth. We can become victims of habit because that makes us feel secure. The daily rituals that are held so dearly become so engrained in us that the thought of changing them is a very scary task. In addition, that routine we have established does not stimulate the need for growth, so there is no growth. When we do not grow, we die.

The one constant in this world is that change is always occurring; it is a part of evolution. The inability to adapt to change seems to creep into our lives as we age, making life an almost robotic experience. That doesn't sound too exciting to me and I don't plan on living mine that way. You are too old to change, you say? Don't believe it for a minute. There are plenty of people who have achieved great things in the twilight of their lives. Writing this book is a first for me. It may or may not sell millions, but achieving the goal and checking it off my bucket list is a huge accomplishment for me and you can do the same. Set some goals, add a little challenge to your life, and you will be amazed at how vibrant your world will become.

> *I don't believe in aging. I believe in forever altering one's aspect to the sun.*
> —Virginia Woolfe

The one celebrity who simply brings a smile to my face when I think of her is Betty White. My goodness, the energy and enthusiasm for life that woman has! At the time of this writing, she is 91 years old and still performing. At age 88, she became the oldest person to host *Saturday Night Live*. She currently has two sitcoms and does bit appearances all the time. She is simply an amazing example of how to get the most out of life.

How you age is up to you. Your body doesn't have to be soft and flabby—get up and move; challenge your mind—read a book; challenge your muscles and your heart and you will receive the best gift you could imagine—growth: mental, physical, emotional, and spiritual. It may not be possible to run a seven-minute mile at age seventy five, but you could begin by walking a few blocks. Each little improvement we add to our lives adds life. Granted, if you are afflicted with physical trials, you can still take the higher road and choose to deal with the ailment in a manner that will improve who you are. Don't focus your attention on the pain, count your blessings, and be grateful you are alive to feel the pain. Though your body may not be able to improve, your attitude can; and when you improve your attitude, life becomes a little better. Imagine how much better life would be if you approached all the challenges you have like this! Getting up each morning would be a joy instead of a task.

I love the Colonel Sanders' story. At age 10, he acquired his first job working on a nearby farm for $2 a month. At age 12, his family moved to another town and he was forced to find another farm to work for. After that, he had a series of jobs. He was a railroad fireman, studied law by correspondence, practiced in justice-of-the-peace courts, sold insurance, operated an Ohio River steamboat ferry, sold tires, and ran service stations. When he was 40, the Colonel began cooking for hungry travelers who stopped at his service station. He didn't have a restaurant then, but served folks on his own dining table in the living quarters of the station. It was in the small town of Corbin, Indiana that the Colonel developed the recipe for that "finger lickin' good" chicken we are all so familiar with today. His fame was spreading.

But as fate would have it, the growth of our country was expanding and a new highway was slated to bypass his little town in Indiana. He could see the writing on the wall. It was time for a change. He decided to auction off all his equipment and settle up his debts, which left him with nothing but his social security check to live on.

At age 62, he was about to begin again. He knew that he had something special with his recipe, so he got in his car and went from town to town franchising his "golden egg" for a nickel a chicken and sealed each deal with a handshake. Over the next 12 years, he signed up over 600 franchises and then sold the entire operation for over $2,000,000. Back in 1964, that was a ton of money. So what did he do then? Sit back and relax, give in and retire? Not the Colonel—he remained the spokesperson for Kentucky Fried Chicken until 1976 and finally retired at the age of 86.

I cannot go back and ask Colonel Sanders what was his motivation for all he achieved late in life, but I am sure that every person who refuses to give in to the death sentence some of us associate with getting old has similar motives.

It was my great pleasure to interview Ruth, a great lady I work with as a realtor to discover her viewpoints that keep her running at full capacity in her golden years. I have never asked Ruth how old she is, and out of respect, no one else at the office has either. Let's just say she is a miraculous example of how to keep life vital and vibrant.

When the sun rises, it does so long after Ruth has woken up. She begins her day with a morning prayer and a routine of exercise. She nourishes her body with healthy food, makes sure her house is in order and then gets dressed for success, preparing herself for a day of helping people with their housing needs. She arrives at the office before it opens and stays for at least eight hours, or until her work for the day is completed.

> *You're never too old, never too bad, never too late, and never too sick to start from scratch once again.*
> —Harriet Morgan

Ruth has many clients and is consistently on the phone answering their many questions. You may find her touring homes, meeting with clients, or in technology classes, seminars or other places that will stimulate her mind. If she doesn't know the answer to a question, she asks; if she needs help solving a problem, she will seek out how to solve it; and if she makes a mistake, she fesses up and apologizes. Ruth's ability to live in the moment is an inspiration, procrastination is not a part of who this woman is.

I asked her what her reason was for getting out of bed each day and her answer was that it was habit. But unlike the habits that can get you in a rut and stagnate growth, Ruth's habit is to learn and grow and make the best of each and every day. Does she worry? Not really. What she cannot control, she does not take the responsibility for, so no worries there. What she can control, she can fix; so no worries there either. What about anger? Her thoughts are that if you let someone anger you, then you are allowing them to own a part of you. It is much more desirable to accept the situation and then move on.

Is Ruth ever fearful? Sometimes she feels fear, but only for fifteen seconds or so. She says she doesn't like that feeling so she must figure out a way to get rid of it. Her advice to those who feel insecure is to conquer one thing at a time. It doesn't have to be a big thing, just one leading you in the direction of confidence. If you gain enough small victories, the insecurity fades.

Ruth does not complain, but counts her blessings instead. She may not be famous, but she is certainly encourages me that life can be worth living, no matter how old you are!

Life is a gift God has given us. When you are given a gift, you should always say thank you. Honoring the giver by taking care of your present and utilizing it to the best of your ability is all He is asking us to do. Age gracefully.

Depression

Depression

Depression demands attention. If left to express itself completely, it can kill you. It is defined as a persistent feeling of sadness and loss of interest. It can affect how you feel, think, and sometimes your physical health.

There is a difference between depression and a simple case of "the blues." The blues tend to be a short-term condition, whereas depression tends to affect the state of your everyday life. You may have trouble functioning in your daily routine and even the simplest of tasks become so overwhelming they cannot be done. Depression can lead you down the path to feeling that life is no longer valuable because you have nothing significant to contribute. Depression can sometimes lead to thoughts of ending your life.

When the chains that bind you become so overpowering that you cannot see a way out, you are experiencing depression. The medical field suggests antidepressants to overcome depression, but all the meds do is mask the problems or cause. Those pills don't cure— they simply create an addiction to the medication. So now not only are you battling a depressed state, but you are reliant on pills to lift your spirits.

Some folks rely on alcohol to numb the pain they feel, or worse yet, street drugs. If these solutions look familiar to you, then I suggest there might be some thought you need to take for a better and more permanent solution to change those disempowering feelings. I am no expert by any means, but I do know that each individual experiencing depression has a unique story that brought him or her to that point in the person's development.

Depression may be caused by chemical imbalances in the body, which may be helped by a simple diet change. It may be caused by a traumatic event in the past or present life, or a history within the family or giving birth (postpartum depression). There are many ways a person can become depressed. This is a very serious, life-threatening condition that needs to be treated by an expert in the field. The downward spiral is much more dangerous and difficult to overcome and professional help will help you focus turning your life around.

Michael Jackson

Michael Jackson was one of the biggest and most talented performers that this generation has ever seen. He possessed what most of humanity appears to want in life—he was unbelievably talented and had more money than he knew what to do with. But, he did not have happiness because on the inside, he carried the heavy burden of depression.

Jackson was born in Gary, Indiana, to a father who worked in a steel plant and a stay-at-home mother who was in charge of nine other children as well. His father had always dreamed of a huge musical career for himself, and when that did not happen, he planned on achieving his dream through his children. It has been reported that he was a strict and abusive person to his family. He pushed and pushed his children to devote their lives to becoming a musical success by constant practice, leaving no room for anything else in their lives.

Michael was five years old when his success began. He was never allowed to experience what it was to develop and grow as other children do. He became sort of a robot controlled by his father's ambition.

Over time and as Michael became a man, those deep, dark memories of his elusive childhood surfaced, causing him to feel there was a part of his life that was missing. It was hard for him to convey this void in his life to others because he felt that no one would understand and almost everyone else had been able to experience the pleasures of childhood. As his fame and success grew, he lavished his attention on children, trying to make up for the childhood he did not have when he was young. But he could not change the past.

As his depression grew, he began trying to ease the pain through drugs and alcohol, which his entourage and paid-for doctors were eager to oblige—if Michael was happy, their lives were good. It was as if there wasn't anyone who really cared about him enough to help him find a real solution to his depression. Relying on people who benefit financially from solving one's problems is not a very trustworthy undertaking. Michael's talent was huge, his success was huge, and so was his growing depression. The drugs and alcohol never seemed to be enough to block out the darkness within

> *That's the thing about depression: A human being can survive almost anything, as long as she sees the end in sight. But depression is so insidious, and it compounds daily, that it's impossible to ever see the end. The fog is like a cage without a key.*
> —Elizabeth Wurtzel

Jackson, so he would take more and more to mask the pain.

Everyone knows how his story ends. But it didn't have to end that way. If he had reached out to the proper channels, he might have gotten true help with his depression.

Managing the dangerous state of depression can be done by just taking the first, small step in faith to begin positive change. Halt the cycle, step off the merry-go-round and gain control of your thoughts. Decide to have peace. Make a plan and figure out the steps that will get you there. Enlist the help of a trusted professional; if that one doesn't work, find another, get a second opinion, get a third. *DO NOT GIVE UP*. It is possible to overcome depression. God didn't make "no junk" and He put you here for a reason. Find it and live it.

When you start building momentum, little by little, life will improve for you, your energy level will increase, and people will take notice of the more vibrant person you are becoming. This change will help you to continue your journey toward freeing yourself from the crippling chains that bound you in the past and kept you from a life of freedom.

Bruce Springsteen

There was a boy who was born in a small town in New Jersey to a blue-collar family. The mother worked as a secretary, and the father bounced around from job to job, never really finding his true purpose in life. Dad often experienced bouts of depression and frequently took out his frustration on his son, while his mother would be the intermediary, trying to keep peace in her family. The father would come home from work, turn off all the lights in the house, and sit in the dark with his six pack of beer and smoke cigarettes at the kitchen table.

If one of the children were to turn on a light, all hell would break loose. So the young son sat in the dark across the table from his father while he grilled the young boy about his future. This often ended in screaming matches with physical skirmishes that pushed the son to run out of the house. The meager household was filled with confrontation and discouraging remnants of what life was about. That was the life that shaped the young boy and who he would become—meet "The Boss," Bruce Springsteen.

In his teen years in the 1960s, Springsteen was led to music as an outlet for the inner turmoil that raged inside him. Because of his memories of his father's battle with depression, he never experimented with drugs when others did. He knew that he was a product of his father and the apple did not fall far from the tree. Springsteen's outlet to ease the sadness he felt about his past was channeled into his musical efforts, making him one of the most talented songwriters and performers we have come to know. His work ethic is extremely demanding and all those who work with him are expected to perform at the same level of intensity. He belts out tune after tune in his lengthy concerts with all the passion he can fathom, releasing the hurt and pain inside.

As time passed and "The Boss" went about living his life, he realized that his father's demons were all too present inside of him and they must be dealt with. He did seek out the support of professionals to help him understand what was happening inside him and how he could convert those disempowering feelings into a meaningful purpose for his life.

That is the key; you cannot change what has happened in the past, but you can change what will happen in your future.

> There's nothing, repeat, nothing to be ashamed of when you're going through a depression. If you get help, the chances of your licking it are really good. But, you have to get yourself onto a safe path.
> —Mike Wallace

So out of the ashes of his childhood rose a greatly talented man who conveys the angst he felt as a young boy. It is his mission in life to tell others that no matter what pain you have had, it does not have to define the person you are. Finding that purpose of why God has put you here will save your life.

Finding answers to depression is not an easy or enjoyable journey. It can take years of therapy to understand the origin of the pain, and even when you do start to make sense of it all, the battle is ongoing. Springsteen was in therapy for over thirty years to ensure that he was winning the war, not just the battle.

The ability to have joy in your heart is an indescribable gift that God gives to us, but sometimes finding it is a task that requires more introspection than can be coped with on our own. Depression is a very complex mental state that originates from our own distinct experiences and can require a myriad of different treatments.

There is not a one-size-fits-all solution to depression because there are so many types of mental conditions that can cause it. Each person must find the treatment that is best suited to help the condition from which he or she suffers. The most important thing one can and must do is to seek out the help of a professional and remember to *NEVER GIVE UP*.

Don't Worry, Be Happy

Don't Worry, Be Happy

Are you thinking, "That's crazy! If I don't focus on what could go wrong, how will I ever fix the problems when they come up? Focusing on solutions to what could possibly go wrong will help me feel prepared and safe."

If that is what comes to mind when you read *"Don't Worry, Be Happy!"* it is time to make a change, a shift in your focus. I would define worry as spending excessive time thinking of all the ways something could go wrong. The more you do it, the larger the trap becomes. When you worry, the images and thoughts upon which you focus create a negative emotional attachment to the issue about which you are feeling anxiety. Trying to move in a positive direction becomes more and more difficult; worry closes you off from growing.

As human beings, we all have the same basic needs that drive us to do the things we do—we either are trying to avoid pain, or moving toward gaining pleasure.

> *If you deliberately plan to be less than you are capable of being, then I warn you that you'll be unhappy for the rest of your life.*
> —Abraham Maslow

The object that is the center of your worry may be a real or perceived concern, one that can generate all sorts of road blocks to stop you from moving toward pleasure.

Worriers tend to live their lives focused on avoiding pain, which ironically causes more pain, because they are cutting off the possibility of gaining pleasure. People who worry excessively are headed toward a more severe state of mind called depression, or even paranoia.

I am not saying you should never worry; I am saying that if you do have a concern that is disturbing to you, focus your attention on a solution that will ease the pain of the threat; not on what will happen if the threat continues. Shift your thought pattern in a new direction that adds a fresh perspective. This will widen the field of vision and will move you forward rather than cut you off from having a positive growth experience.

Howard Hughes

Howard Hughes was an extraordinary business man who, from the outside looking in, had the life that everyone wished for. At age eighteen, he inherited his father's oil drill manufacturing business. He took his inheritance and invested it in making movies and became even richer. Howard was handsome, rich, and seemed to have it all. He earned the reputation as a playboy in the rich and famous circuit. By all appearances, he was a success.

Inside, Mr. Hughes was another story, one that he kept to himself and became a growing obsession. You see,

Howard worried constantly that he would catch some sort of disease if he did not protect himself from germs. The older he got, the more obsessed he became, until finally, he became a total recluse to avoid germs.

After a severe plane crash in 1946, he began his downward spiral into isolation. He was rarely seen in public after that and it was rumored that his constant worry about disease led him to the conclusion that he had no control over all aspects of his life.

> *Every thought is a seed. If you plant crabapples, don't count on harvesting Golden Delicious.*
> —Bill Meyer

Today, we call this behavior obsessive-compulsive and would have been able to help him overcome some of his anxiety. Worry destroyed Howard Hughes' world.

The source of a person's worries most likely comes from lack of confidence they feel because of some event or person taking their power away. It can begin in early childhood by well-meaning parents who want the best for their child, but feels that they need to control every outcome leaving the child powerless to make their own choices.

When such children grow up and become adults, they will worry about what choices to make because they have been conditioned by their parents to believe that their decisions are not to be trusted. These adult children do not know how to proceed and worry that if they make a choice and the outcome is bad, they will feel badly. The cycle contin-ues until those people decide enough is enough. When that moment comes, change can occur. If only Mr. Hughes could have recognized his moment of truth, rather than obsess about his lack of control over germs.

Change can be difficult, but it is simple to do. Decide. Make a choice. The states of being I write about in this book—fear, anger, shame and so on—

can all be changed with a simple decision to change. The difficult part of change is deciding to do it. Where people run into trouble is when they try to change the world all at once.

Change does not happen instantly. It takes persistence and is done one step at a time. Think about the age-old question, "How do you eat an elephant?" ... "One bite at a time."

You do not have to make change an enormous task that is next to impossible to achieve. Take little steps in overcoming your negative affliction. If you worry that the weather will deter you from doing something, it will. Do it anyway and appreciate the process. Pat yourself on the back when you make progress. You are moving toward overcoming a fear. The world is becoming a little brighter and you are feeling a tad better.

Time for the next step: tackle another fear. Remember that controlling parent who created feelings of inadequacy in you? Do something that will build up your confidence and help tear down that illusionary wall of fear that is inside you. It can be as simple as starting up a conversation with a complete stranger. You may worry that the stranger will dismiss you. So what? What is the worst thing that can happen? You might be rejected, but the best thing that can happen is that you know you tried. If it is something that you have been taught to fear, then facing it and taking action will counteract that fear. Again, pat yourself on the back, you have made progress.

Now you are creating momentum, and with momentum, you are creating the change you want. Each successful step you take will build your confidence and before you know it, your worries will be a thing of the past.

Edith Bunker

The 1970s brought us a cutting-edge television sitcom called *All in the Family* that tackled the issues of racism and bigotry of its era. In the cast, Edith Bunker, the brow-beaten wife, was married to Archie Bunker, the bigot.

Edith always lived in fear of what Archie thought and worried constantly about what would make him happy. Mostly she would oblige and give him what he wanted if that did not conflict with her own inner compass.

When Edith's core values were jeopardized, however, she would DECIDE to react differently, more in line with her own beliefs. Was she afraid to stand up for herself? Most likely the answer is yes. Did she worry about what Archie would say or do? I am sure the answer is yes. Did the worry help relieve the stress of the situation? No, it did not. Contrarily it probably added to the stressfulness. Did she receive satisfaction from the decision to stand up for herself? Most likely, the answer is yes.

Nothing good comes from worry; it cannot change anything. The only result you will receive from worrying is stress that harms your physical body and can create debilitating health conditions; or mentally, it can lead you to paranoia and depression. Neither outcome solves anything.

The one thing that can help you live through trouble in peace is faith; for me personally, that is faith in God.

In 2007, the economy was at its highest and everyone was flying high, myself included. As a realtor, I was enjoying the benefits of a booming economy, selling property left and right. Anyone who breathed could get a mortgage. The downward shift began the end of that year. The economy slowed, major financial institutions fell, and the downward spiral of our inflated lifestyles was headed for disaster.

At that time, I owned several properties and had taken second mortgages on all of them, leaving no equity in any of the properties. As a realtor, I should have known better, but I never anticipated that the money train would stop. It came to a screeching halt. I had no income and exorbitant expenses. That, my friends, is where I learned how to worry.

Bill collectors calling, sleepless nights, the sick feeling in my stomach, and the shame of my situation were all a part of my everyday life back then. I couldn't believe I had to worry about losing my house or that my car could be taken away. For a while, I got by on borrowed money, which only made matters worse. I even became reclusive at times and depression had set in.

One day in the early fall, I decided to take a ride to the beach of Lake Michigan and go for a shoreline walk. As the torment twisted and turned inside me, the consistent crashing of the waves on shore began to calm my heart. When I neared the end of my walk, I lay down on the beach with my eyes closed and started talking to God. The clear air, warm sun, and crashing waves seemed to consume me as I prayed for a solution to the mess I was in. I asked God for a sign—and there it was.

When I opened my eyes, the clouds seemed to be surrounding me. It was as if I could reach my hand up and touch them, that's how close they appeared to me. I felt a new sense of peace inside me, telling me that everything was going to be OK, trust me. From that day forward, I no longer worried about what was to be. I knew that if I did my best, that would be enough.

I tell you this not to employ your sympathy, but to share a truth that took me a long time to discover: worry solves nothing! It wasn't until I decided to change my focus that my life began to improve. I have learned a lot in the past few years and I am happy to tell you that it doesn't matter how bad you perceive your problems to be, you can be happy with the choices you make to resolve them.

Was it easy to overcome my financial debacle? No, it was quite difficult, but the solution was simple: just take action, make a change for the good, and life gets better.

From Insecurity to Confidence

From Insecurity
to Confidence

Maybe this chapter should have been named from confidence to insecurity because when we are born, we know no insecurity. It is from the environment in which we live that insecurities are developed. The only thing we know before our birth is the security of our mother's womb.

So how do you get from there to here? Try to imagine yourself trapped in a deteriorating marriage, experiencing lack of self-worth and filled with feelings of inadequacy. Take a minute and close your eyes and really feel those feelings. When you first met your husband or wife, you did not feel that way, so what has happened over the years to cause this insecurity? Remember in the beginning how exciting it was when the phone rang and you saw his or her number? The anticipation of the connection that made you gush with happiness started to flood your being, and you could hardly wait to answer the call.

A new relationship is a period of discovery where finding out all the personal little details about one another is the most fascinating way to spend time you could fathom. Each little nugget of intimacy discovered brings the joy of becoming closer, or knowing that person more intimately. The interest you show in the other person is a gift you are giving the other, making him or her feel good about you so the feeling is reciprocated and the relationship grows. As the relationship continues to blossom, the confidence in the solidity of the commitment grows as well. Each day, you are more secure with your new-found feelings of love.

Now you might think that we as humans would be satisfied with that and be grateful for the grand reward that has been bestowed upon us for connecting positively with another person— but that is when we sabotage ourselves. Feeling secure with the love you now have with this person sometimes will lead to complacency when it comes to continuing to develop the connection that you have. After all, you now know this person and what you know makes you totally happy, so why shouldn't you focus attention on other areas of your life? Wouldn't that expand your happiness? Those areas of growth might be career, or a sporting interest, or a myriad of other choices.

When you choose to do that instead of focusing your attention on the relationship, you are separating yourself from the love that has recently been discovered. That separation will stop the growth. You might turn your attention to a project at work and stay later at the office a few times a week, or cancel dinner plans because your friends asked you to attend a sporting event with them. Whatever the case may be, putting your spouse or significant other in second place makes that person less significant in your life at that moment. This is when insecurity can arise in a relationship, allowing doubt and fear to rear their ugly selves and disrupt the harmony you strived so hard to create.

The need to feel secure is a need we all have, and when that need is no longer met, feelings of resentment and/or inadequacy can develop, leading to trouble in our relationships. It may not be your primary need in life, but it may be the primary need of the person of significance with who you are in relationship. When that need is not satisfied, insecurities will arise and thus the relationship may begin to deteriorate.

> *If one advances confidently in the direction of his dreams, and endeavors to live the life which he has imagined, he will meet with success unexpectedly in common hours.*
> —Henry David Thoreau

Ironically, discovering the unknown things about your partner when you first met or the things you were uncertain about, is no longer a process of importance to you. In the beginning, that uncertainty was exciting. You were learning and growing, which stimulated another need in your life—the need to grow. The need to grow can create confidence in a person as well, if growth is a need key to who you are.

Both security and growth are part of each of us, but they are not necessarily ranked in the same order because we are all put together differently. You might feel the need to be significant more than

> *It's insecurity that is always chasing you and standing in the way of your dreams.*
> —Vin Diesel

I do and I might feel the need to grow is more important to me than it is to you. Both needs can invoke confidence, just not at the same level in each of us. The trick is to recognize the primary need in others and make sure to contribute to that need in a positive way, which will instill a feeling of confidence in the other person.

Insecurity. We know what it is: the opposite of being secure or confident. The question that needs answering is why do we feel insecure? The experiences each of us has during the course of a lifetime are like our own intricate jigsaw puzzle. When we begin to put together all the unique pieces, an image will begin to appear and that image is who we have become. Some of the pieces of a life may have been dark, foreboding experiences: a bully, a condescending parent, or an unfamiliar circumstance we find ourselves in. Or it might be as simple as a statement made to us a long time ago.

Once the "why" becomes apparent, then figuring out how to overcome the insecurity becomes more real to us, Now we have something solid on which to develop a solution. As in overcoming anything, what is focused on is what we will get in life. Shifting focus is the cornerstone of change. Once we get that concept, the possibilities opening up before us will be endless.

If you are lost, hungry, and sitting in the middle of a desert, you most likely will not be very secure about the situation because you do not have any experiences that can be referred to for help. Lack of personal experience will almost always invoke insecurity. So what would make it possible for you to develop confidence in an unfamiliar situation as this?

The first step would be to familiarize yourself with the surroundings and find any resources that are available to you. Is there a highway nearby? Where is the sun so you can determine direction? What food and water resources are there? As you uncover each small detail that may remedy the problem, you will gain confidence and begin to overcome the insecurity you felt prior to obtaining this knowledge.

The next step would be to compile all the information you have discovered and develop a plan utilizing those resources. By being in charge of what you focus on alone will help improve the current situation. You will gain confidence that you are moving in the right direction, which will stimulate your brain to look for more resources and solutions. This is developing a pattern and building momentum. Momentum is the component that will drive this plan of yours to a successful outcome.

Now that confidence is beginning to overcome your insecurities, be careful that you do not become complacent. Keep that momentum moving you forward. Remember to be persistent in your efforts and patient with your progress. Before you know it, you will be headed out of the predicament. Soon the freedom of a successful journey out of the desert will be yours.

Strangely enough, both insecurity and confidence are forces that can motivate people to grow. When insecurity becomes so uncomfortable that the choice to change that feeling is an absolute must, the focus will shift to a new direction and growth will happen. When confidence of some knowledge you have in a specific area becomes a part of who you are, you have developed the courage to take on new things that prior to obtaining that confidence, you would never have attempted.

The Wizard of Oz

The best example I can give you of insecurity comes from the great timeless story of *The Wizard of Oz*. We have all seen this extremely creative film that portrays Dorothy and her dog, the Scarecrow, the Tin Man, and the Cowardly Lion as having insecurities of one sort or another. Dorothy is fearful that she may never get back to her home in Kansas. The Scarecrow fears that he is not smart enough to navigate life on his own, (*"if I only had a brain...."*). The Tin Man thinks he is incapable of caring for anyone and fears never finding love (*"if I only had a heart..."*). And probably the most fearful of all is the Cowardly Lion who lacks any sign of confidence what so ever (*"if I only had courage..."*).

When these four meet up on the yellow brick road, they start talking about this wonderful place called Emerald City, or the Land of Oz, where life is rosy and all things are possible. Once they agree that this is the place they need to go, they set out on a quest to get to Oz no matter how hard the journey is.

During the course of their adventure, they are attacked by the Wicked Witch of the West who puts them through all sorts of perils and compromising situations, but they manage to overcome anything she throws at them. They are gaining confidence, but do not realize it.

Finally the reach the Land of Oz and meet up with the magical Wizard who gives the Scarecrow a degree stating he is smart, the Tin Man receives a symbolic heart, and the Cowardly Lion receives a medal of courage to cure his insecurity. The Wizard is still at a loss on how to get Dorothy back to Kansas, though. Finally grasping at straws, he tells her to put on the ruby red slippers, close her eyes and click her heels together three times and she will be transported back to her beloved family in Kansas. Luckily, because it is a dream, it works, and she and her little dog Toto are whisked away and she finds herself in bed at home with all her loved ones around her.

We all know that these characters achieved their confidence on their own by making good decisions on their journey to the Emerald City and the Wizard of Oz. They perceived the answer to their insecurities to be receiving validation from a higher authority which is what the Wizard gave them. That was their "Aha" moment. They had grown into the characters that they had so desperately desired to be.

Growth is life. We all need to grow in order to get the most out of life, so turn off the TV and pick up a book. Step away from the refrigerator and go for a walk. Do something to nourish your soul and give it new experiences. This satisfies both your need to grow from your insecurities and your need to be confident that these actions will improve your life. Any state of being you may find yourself in can be utilized in a positive way, if you approach it with intent to improve the situation. Change your ways and you will change your life.

Great + Attitude = Gratitude

Great + Attitude = Gratitude

L iving with gratitude makes our world a better place. Gratitude is the art of thankfulness, the ability to appreciate each moment and experience it as if it were a miracle (it is, you know) or as they say, "counting your blessings." Living with gratitude can improve your health, reduce the stress you feel, increase your happiness, and improve your relationships. Gratitude is a pretty important life-changer, one that everyone should consider.

You might think that just deciding to be grateful cannot be the real answer of how to live with gratitude—that is too simple. Just like most of the choices in this book, it is simple and easy, once you choose to live with an "attitude of gratitude." Maybe not at first, but as with all new ideas, the more you practice it, the better you become at it. The biggest hurdle to overcome is arriving at the decision to change the manner in which you approach life. Once you set the direction, the rest will follow.

The best example I can give you on finding a life filled with gratitude is from the story *A Christmas Carol* by Charles Dickens. Yep, I am talking about our old friend Scrooge. He was a selfish man, the total opposite of living with gratitude. He was grateful for nothing and by living his life in that manner, his world was confined to his work. He ignored his family, treated his employees badly, and was a miserable, old soul. Finally the Big Guy upstairs said enough was enough. Scrooge was out of control and it was time to give him a "do over" and then a makeover. He sent down some help for poor ol' Scrooge and that is when He commissioned three spirits to visit him to teach him the attitude of gratitude.

His first visit was from the Ghost of his Past. Past Ghost took him into his history, dredging up all the hurts and pain that caused Scrooge to shut down and cut off relationships with all that was good in his life. This experience made him open his heart and feel those necessary emotions again. You see, it wasn't the emotions that crippled him, but the choices he made in response to the pain.

Pain can bring you to your knees, and when that happens, you choose to either deal with it in the most positive way you can, or you hide from it. Scrooge's choice was to cut himself off from the source of the pain to avoid it—never a good idea and not really a fix to the problem.

The second ghost to visit Scrooge was Ghost of the Present. Her mission was to reveal to him what his world looked like from the outside. He saw an angry old man treating everyone badly. He chose to work his life away, ignoring any involvement with relationships. This time, when his heart opened, he felt the fear he disguised with pride and selfishness in his everyday life.

Isn't that what we do when we avoid having relationship, hide in our own little world to dodge the discomfort we feel? It takes a concerted effort to make connection with others, which is difficult to face if you have become trapped in yourself. Do it anyway. All relationships have problems at some point. Choosing to meet those challenges with courage and integrity will help you grow your life and give you peace and joy about who you are. Scrooge had no joy in his life.

Lastly, a visit from Future Ghost pointed out what Scrooge's life would look like in the future. He was brought to witness his demise and saw that no one came to show respect for him because he was not loved in his life. This last visit opened his heart to feel the dread and even more fear. The lesson was to illustrate that if one's focus is self-directed, then that is exactly what will happen at in the end—to be alone and by yourself.

To have love in your life, you must also give love. Once you give love, you attract love, because when you give love, you begin to feel love of whom you are and that will make you happy. Everyone likes to be around those who radiate joy.

Because Scrooge's heart had been opened up by the three spirits, he was now able to appreciate his relationships and approached life in a positive and humble way. He was grateful for each and every moment he had left on the face of this planet. He was a changed man, looking for love in all the right places with a heart of gratitude.

> Gratitude unlocks the fullness of life. It turns what we have into enough, and more. It turns denial into acceptance, chaos to order, confusion to clarity. It can turn a meal into a feast, a house into a home, a stranger into a friend.
> —Melody Beattie

Until this review, I never realized the depth of this story's meaning and how it relates to the condition of human beings. When you live life with gratitude, miracles will pop up every day for you. Life is nicer and you become more vibrant and alive.

Which Scrooge would you like to be—the before or after?

The moment you open your eyes in the morning is a reason to feel grateful. Taking that first conscious breath is a reason to feel grateful. If you set aside a few minutes each morning to acknowledge the things in your life you feel gratitude for, you will be a little happier throughout the day. Be thankful for the little things that you might take for granted. If your furnace is broken, be thankful that you have a house with a furnace. If you are having trouble at work, be thankful that you have a job and the opportunity to solve the problem.

How you approach your daily life affects not only yourself, but everyone else around you. Wouldn't you rather spread happiness and feelings of joy rather than denying the people you care about that beautiful gift? When someone does something kind for you, tell that person thank you. If he or she is not physically present, pick up the phone and give a quick call, send an email, send a text—send out the happiness you feel for the kind gesture. Not only will you make the other person feel happy and appreciated, you will reap the rewards of happiness as well. You will be grateful for the act of kindness you just did.

The Dalai Lama, the Tibetan spiritual and temporal leader, teaches that living a life in gratitude strengthens relationships among people. By living life through loving others, compassionate feelings for all humankind and peaceful resolution to differences, he has earned the respect of the world. I will not try to interpret his great teachings, so I will give you his universal philosophy from the acceptance of the Nobel Peace Prize his own words:

>*"The need for simple*
>*human-to-human relationships*
>*is becoming increasingly*
>*urgent...*

*Today the world is smaller
and more interdependent.
One nation's problems can no
longer be solved by itself
completely. Thus, without a
sense of universal responsibility, our very survival
becomes threatened. Basi-
cally, universal responsibility
is feeling for other people's
suffering just as we feel our
own. It is the realization that
even our enemy is entirely
motivated by the quest for
happiness. We must recognize
that all beings want the same
thing that we want. This is
the way to achieve a true
understanding, unfettered by
artificial consideration."*

I would like to share my personal experience of what brought gratitude into my
life because I feel it may be the same
lesson that so many of us could have or

experience. The economic downturn humbled me and brought me to my knees. Prior to the turn of events, I would snub my nose at discount stores and had to have all the designer brands; go out to dinner three or four times a week; vacation often and basically buy anything I wanted. I didn't appreciate what I had and it didn't seem to make me happy either. It wasn't until the income went away— and the bills did not— that my attention turned to my immediate situation.

> *Acknowledging the good that you already have in your life is the foundation for all abundance.*
> —Eckhart Tolle

When the phone rang, I feared it could be a mortgage company, credit card company, or a utility company looking for payment from me. I had no money to pay these bills and lived in constant fear and anxiety because of this. Would they foreclose on my house or would they take my car for lack of payment? That way of life and living with fear went on for several years. As I look back to that very scary time in my life, I realize that God brought me there to help me see what is really important in life. Being scared of what I could lose made me appreciate what I had.

When I began to feel that gratitude for all the resources around me, my life began to change. My focus started to go from dwelling in the pain of the current environment of lack to how to solve my sad, financial condition. With a lot of hard work and thoughtful planning, I was able to set a course that would steer me in the right direction. It was very difficult and painful to do, but little by little, I was able to dig my way out of debt and save my life. I learned how very precious all the things were that I almost lost. Now I treat everything and everyone in my life with the upmost respect and am very thankful that I was blessed with the ability to find a way to keep them.

Do you want to know the irony in this experience for me? I am so much happier now than I was back before I experienced this life transformation. I wake up each day with a smile on my face and go through my day with a bounce in my step, because in my heart I know that I have abundance in my life. I am grateful.

Be grateful for everything and everyone in the world. If you have knowledge that may help make a life easier, be grateful for it and then share it. Maybe you have acquired financial success—be grateful to those who helped you achieve it, say thank you, be generous, and share the good fortune with others. An attitude of gratitude blesses the world.

Sharing the Joy

Sharing the Joy

Feeling joy is the ultimate reward for overcoming fear, shame, discouragement, or any other negative states of being. It is the gift that we are all striving to achieve with our lives. Joy is different from happiness—happiness is more of a temporary feeling that can come and go with the events in your life, while being joyful is a state that is a part of who you are because of the way you conduct your life.

Life is going to have its ups and downs and we know that being happy about the down times is not the usual response. However, we may feel extreme gratitude that we are equipped with the necessary implements to handle those down times. The joy of knowing we are capable is imbedded in our being as confidence.

Are you beginning to see how all these positive attributes—joy, happiness, gratitude—are interwoven? When you achieve a breakthrough in one state, it often leads you to another empowering emotion, thus creating a new and more dynamic you.

Please remember that momentum also works against you when you are trapped in negative states, as we discovered in the previous chapter on depression. Fear of coping with something can also create shame because you are not facing the fear. If you accept shame in your life, then that may depress you. On and on it can go until you decide to do something about it and make a change. The best moment of a life can be when you hit rock bottom and the pain can no longer be tolerated. You decide enough is enough and that is when your thought process will shift from being closed off and isolated from the joy of life to one that will figure out how to make it better. The moment you shift your focus to finding a solution to ease the pain is the first step toward a better life.

Robin Roberts

Robin Roberts is a co-host on *Good Morning America* and has publicly shared some of her most painful experiences as they were happening. In 2007, Roberts discovered a lump in her breast and was diagnosed with breast cancer. As she battled through the treatment, she was open and candid about her feelings so the viewers could gain a perspective of her way of coping with the illness. As she recovered, little by little, she would feel stronger and that led her to gratitude.

Her story of difficulty continued as several years later she was feeling very tired and decided it was time to find out why. It should have been a joyous time for her as *GMA* had just received the honor of being voted the number one morning show in America and the cast and crew were flying high. After the celebration, Roberts got a call from her physician, receiving the news that she had a grave and serious disease called Mylodisplastic Syndrome (MDS), which is a pre-leukemia disease. Along with this devastating news came the startling life expectancy of a mere eighteen months if left untreated. It was hard for her to wrap her mind around this sequence of events; she was stunned.

Roberts needed a bone marrow donor and asking someone to do something that was such a great sacrifice was a very humbling experience for her. She was always the one who gave and sacrificed, and being a recipient was a position that was unfamiliar to her. Her decision to publicly share her grave life events was very difficult. She worried about how the news would be received and how it would impact those in her life. It took great courage to open her painful world up for all to experience, but Ms. Roberts knew it was the right thing to do.

By the grace of God, her sister Sally Ann turned out to be a perfect match and did not hesitate to volunteer for this very difficult and painful procedure. In preparing for the surgery, Roberts had to go through very intense sessions of chemotherapy to wipe out her entire immune system so she could receive the stem cells to replace the defective ones that currently occupied her body. As the treatment happened, it put her in a very vulnerable state and Roberts was placed in isolation, as sterile an environment as possible.

One month before the bone marrow transplant was to be performed, her mother's health began to deteriorate and she was about to die. Roberts left the hospital and her treatment to see her mom for one last time, then it was back to the hospital and treatment. The surgery was getting closer and all precautions needed to be heeded. Roberts had plenty of time to reflect on her life because of the long periods of isolation. As the date of the surgery grew closer, she made a decision to view it as a celebration of the doctors giving her the gift of life and God's guiding their every move.

When the procedure was done and her recovery complete, Roberts took the time to grieve for her mother's death. The very emotional turmoil she faced in the recent past was made available to her family, friends and fans by the transparency she had created for them.

> *Joy does not simply happen to us. We have to choose joy and keep choosing it every day.*
> —Henri Nouwen

While you may not see the joy in this story, or that the sharing of this story would help make the world a better place, here is the message as quoted by Roberts: "*Out of the messes that happen in a life comes the message.*" Sharing the message was the divine act that would be her purpose in life to help others.

Many miracles happened along the way that would impact awareness of the disease. Shortly after Roberts was released from care, she attended the Super Bowl in New Orleans, just a short jaunt from where she grew up. Her *GMA* family was very supportive during the entire ordeal of her illness and as the message of her courage and determination grew, so did the desire to raise awareness of MDS. At the Super Bowl, testing areas were set up called "Swabbing for Robin," where testing was performed to determine bone marrow recipients and education of the process. Do you think that may help save some lives in the future?

> *Being happy doesn't mean that everything is perfect. It means that you've decided to look beyond the imperfections.*
> —Anonymous

Robin Roberts wakes up each day with gratitude and joy because she has experienced the stripping away of all pretenses to reveal simple truths, honesty, and her true heart of hearts. The trials she endured became the joy in her life. Walking down the street and feeling a breeze on her face, smelling the familiar scents of everyday life, and all the other simple things that others so often take for granted are sources of joy. We just need to remember that.

Our Creator has made us for a reason and it is our mission in life to figure out what that purpose is and then fulfill it. Living our lives in this world is our journey to discover not only who we are, but also why we are here. There are clues to be found in our quest and they are the gifts that God has given to us.

For me, it was a simple walk in the woods each day. For over 30 years, I have been led to the forest in my quest for answers. It was there that I found my relationship with God. He has healed a broken heart, calmed my anger, and inspired me to be the best I can be. The time I spend just being and appreciating all the beauty that is in this world is worth more to me than anything else. It renews my soul, humbles my heart, and serves as my compass to a better me.

Sharing the joy within me is a path I have been traveling for quite a long time.

There have been a few dead ends, but the learning experiences along the way were part of the journey.

Realizing that life is not going to be perfect is a great relief and takes the pressure of "being perfect" off of you. What can be joyful is the manner in which you conduct your life. Peel away all the layers of pretense to radiate the awesome, incredible soul you are meant to be. Share your joy, live your peace, and love your life.

Capturing joy will add years to your life, create more energy, and inspire new dreams. Your heart will grow bigger and break away the chains so you can experience bliss and complete freedom of the bondage you so diligently work to overcome.

Unchain Your Heart!

About the Author

Linda Dore has reinvented herself and inspired many others in the process. As a successful business-person over the past three decades and as a single mother, she has sought guidance and inspiration from the experiences and legacies of some of the world's great leaders. Linda has learned to reshape her life away from adversity and sometimes despair by taking those teachings and joining them to her own rediscovered spiritual faith. From being inspired by others to being the inspiration to many, Linda has lived the joy of finding new hope.

Linda lives in suburban Chicagoland, while her two daughters and their families live comfortably close by in the Midwest. Learn more about Linda at www.unchainyourheart.net

CPSIA information can be obtained at www.ICGtesting.com
Printed in the USA
LVOW12s1805261013

358656LV00002B/9/P